THE EXTRAORDINARY ORDINARY

Seeing The Magnficent God In The Ordinary

I

DUKE STONE

Copyright © 2024 by Duke Stone

TrinityStone Publishing

All rights reserved.

No part of this book may be reproduced in any form or by any electronic or mechanical means, including information storage and retrieval systems, without written permission from the author, except for the use of brief quotations in a book review.

Scripture quotations, unless otherwise indicated, are taken from the Holy Bible, New Living Translation, copyright © 1996, 2004, 2015 by Tyndale House Foundation. Used by permission of Tyndale House Publishers, Inc., Carol Stream, Illinois 60188. All rights reserved.

Scripture quotations are taken from the Holy Bible, New International Version®, NIV®. Copyright © 1973, 1978, 1984, 2011 by Biblica, Inc.® Used by permission of Zondervan. All rights reserved worldwide. www.zondervan.com The "NIV" and "New International Version" are trademarks registered in the United States Patent and Trademark Office by Biblica, Inc.®

For my wife, Shirlene. You have been my partner in the ministry for over four decades. Thank you for joining me on this incredible journey!

INTRODUCTION

∼

"Jesus always used stories and illustrations like these when speaking to the crowds. In fact, he never spoke to them without using such parables."
(Matthew 13:34)

∼

In Matthew 13:34, we are told that Jesus often used parables and stories to convey profound spiritual truths. These tales were not just simple anecdotes; they were windows into the deeper realities of God's Kingdom. By using everyday situations and familiar scenarios, Jesus made divine truths accessible and relatable to all who listened. Storytelling was His preferred method to reveal the extraordinary God through the ordinary things of life.

My mother subscribed to Reader's Digest magazine. As a young child, I remember eagerly awaiting their arrival each month at our Post Office box. I would read them from cover to cover. The pages were full of short stories, anecdotes, and articles that captured everyday life in amusing and profound ways. Sections like Laughter, the Best Medicine, Humor in Uniform, Drama in Real Life, and Readers' Contribution helped me realize the power of brief stories that usually revealed deep values. This early habit of reading instilled in me a fondness for ordinary moments that hold extraordinary lessons.

"The Extraordinary Ordinary: Seeing the Extraordinary God in the Ordinary Things of Life" is an invitation to join me on this journey. Designed to pull back the spiritual veil a bit, the 90 devotions included in this book will help you see the Divine in the commonplace things of life. Some are drawn from newspaper and magazine articles that, as I read them, sparked a reflection of Him. Some are based on small, seemingly insignificant nuances of the Scriptures themselves, and as I read in my daily devotions, the Holy Spirit nudged me with a varied or insightful thought.

Each devotion is a short story or reflection designed to uncover the extraordinary ways God reveals Himself in our daily lives. I may be wrong, but I sense most of us feel God is playing some game of cosmic Hide-And-Go-Seek, and we are in spiritual pursuit to see if we can find where He is hiding. The problem arises when we are always looking for burning bushes, wrestling angels, or parting waters.

But I believe the opposite is true. I believe God's presence is ever near, waiting to be noticed. Life is full of ordinary moments that, upon closer inspection, reveal God's extraordinary touch. Through these devotions, I hope to encourage you to pause, reflect, and see the hand of God at work in your life. Like the stories from Reader's Digest, these devotions aim to open your eyes to the deeper truths that lie just beneath the surface of everyday life.

1
THE TEARS MEAN HE'S REAL

Jesus wept.
(John 11:35, KJV)

Anyone who has seen Me has seen the Father!
(John 14:9)

For we have not an high priest which cannot be touched with the feeling of our infirmities;
(Hebrews 4:15, KJV)

∽

On the children's TV show Sesame Street, Big Bird had a friend named Snuffleupugus. Because Big Bird was the only one who had seen him, the other characters on the show thought he was an imaginary friend. They finally convinced Big Bird that he needed to say goodbye to his "imaginary friend."

In a heartwarming scene, Big Bird informs Snuffleupugus that they can't be friends anymore because Snuffy is only imaginary. They embrace each other goodbye, and as Big Bird pulls back, he notices tears on his feathers from his friend. He reasons that if the tears are genuine, his friend must be real. [1]

See Jesus weeping at Lazarus' tomb (John 11:35). In a few chapters later, Jesus would say, "Anyone who has seen Me has seen the Father!" (John 14:9) If we want to know what the Father's heart is, look at the heart of Jesus. When we see Jesus weeping, He is telling us the Father weeps with us.

Recall the writer of Hebrews words, "For we have not an high priest which cannot be touched with the feeling of our infirmities" (Hebrews 4:15 KJV). Jesus empathizes with our infirmities and understands our feelings.

When you feel alone, when your heart hurts, and when it feels like no one understands, remember your feelings and touch him. As He did at the tomb of Lazarus, He weeps with us. And never forget: He can change the tears of the tomb into a celebration of life.

Prayer

Dear Jesus, I am thankful that You became flesh and dwelt among us. Because of that, You understand my feelings. I come to You with my burdens, knowing that You are touched by my pain and You are ready to comfort me. When I am broken, I ask you to soothe my heart and bring me peace and hope. Amen.

---

1. Spinney, C., & Milligan, J. (2007). *The wisdom of Big Bird (and the dark genius of Oscar The Grouch): Lessons from a Life in Feathers.* pp. 47-48. Villard.

2
SPROUTING HOPE

"For there is hope of a tree, If it be cut down, that it will sprout again."
(Job 14:7, KJV)

My wife loves willow trees. The grandkids all know it is "grandma's favorite tree." As we drive down the road, they delight in proclaiming, "I see grandma's favorite tree."

When we moved into our last house in Chattanooga several years ago, there was a small stump of a tree sticking out of the ground in the backyard. It was only a stump, and it appeared dead. But soon after we moved in, I noticed sprouts coming out of the stump. I would whack them with the weed-eater, but they would return. One day, I decided just to let them grow. Later, a full-grown willow tree was sitting in our backyard...grandma's favorite tree.

I thought of that tree as I read this verse from Job 14:7-9: *"For there is hope for a tree when it is cut down, that it will sprout again, and its shoots will not fail."* The enemy is a master at cutting down hope in our lives. Events, circumstances, and people can leave us disappointed. The wise man wrote, "Hope deferred makes the heart sick, but a longing fulfilled is a tree of life" (Proverbs 13:12).

But God can give us hope. Hope that what may appear dead today (relationships, finances, health, etc.) can come alive again through His incredible power. He is the Resurrection and Life. He can bring life to our dreams and our hopes.

∼

Prayer

Heavenly Father, thank You for being my God of hope, always shining Your light in my darkest moments. I ask that You bring Your Divine hope to me in desperate situations, lifting my spirit and filling my heart with Your comforting presence. May Your unfailing love and grace renew my strength and guide me through every challenge. Amen.

∼

3
LITTLE IS MUCH

"I tell you the truth, if you had faith even as small as a mustard seed, you could say to this mountain, 'Move from here to there,' and it would move. Nothing would be impossible."
(Matthew 17:20)

"Well done, My good and faithful servant."
(Matthew 25:23)

Can you guess the world's largest producer of tires? Goodyear? Firestone? Michelin? Would it surprise you to know it is…Lego? That's right. The snap-together block company creates over 300 million tires annually for their models.[1]

In a world that often celebrates the extraordinary, it is easy

---

1. Terdiman, D. (2012, April 4). Rolling, rolling, rolling: Lego, the world's biggest tire maker. *CNET*. https://www.cnet.com/culture/rolling-rolling-rolling-lego-the-worlds-biggest-tire-maker/

to overlook the impact of the ordinary. But it shouldn't surprise us that God often anoints the ordinary. Remember Gideon? Let's not forget about the woman who gave her little in the offering yet received a commendation from Jesus. Or the little boy with five loaves and two fish?

Or, how about the mustard seed? Jesus said, "I tell you the truth, if you had faith even as small as a mustard seed, you could say to this mountain, 'Move from here to there,' and it would move. Nothing would be impossible." (Matthew 17:20)

The often repeated examples throughout the Bible of seemingly insignificant people or inadequate resources provide inspiration when we feel unnoticed, insignificant, or unimportant.

Who knows? Perhaps today, God will publicly recognize your previously unnoticed contribution to His Kingdom. And if not today one day, you will hear Him say, "Well done, My good and faithful servant." (Matthew 25:23)

Prayer

Heavenly Father, thank You for recognizing and using ordinary moments and people to accomplish Your extraordinary purposes. Help me to see the value in the ordinary life, knowing that You can transform the mundane into the miraculous. May I trust in Your power to work through my simple acts of faith and obedience, bringing glory to Your name. Amen.

4
WHAT ARE YOU BUILDING

"Work willingly at whatever you do, as though you were working for the Lord rather than for people."
(Colossians 3:23)

Sarah Arthur from the University of Northwestern, Saint Paul, shares an inspiring story about three bricklayers. When asked what they were doing, the first bricklayer said, "I'm laying bricks." The second replied, "I'm building a wall." The third proudly declared, "I'm constructing a cathedral to the glory of God." The perspective of each bricklayer varied, even though their tasks were identical.[1]

We know that while WHAT we do is important, WHY we do it is equally or more important. In Colossians 3:23, Paul

---

[1]. Arthur, Sarah. (February 15, 2024).*Laying bricks or building the kingdom?* University of Northwestern, St. Paul. https://www.unwsp.edu/blog/laying-bricks-or-building-the-kingdom/

writes, "Work willingly at whatever you do, as though you were working for the Lord rather than for people." The Greek word for "willingly" means "from the soul."[2]

Whether laying bricks or building walls, our motivation transforms the mundane into something magnificent... constructing a cathedral for the glory of God.

When we view our daily tasks as acts of worship and service to God, we saturate them with eternal significance. I desire to live my life today, seeing every action as part of a grand design for God's glory.

∼

Prayer

Father, I come to You with a heart full of gratitude and a desire to serve. I submit myself to Your will, asking for a willing heart that is ready to work for Your kingdom. Empower me with Your Spirit so that I may joyfully and faithfully carry out the tasks You set before me, always seeking to glorify Your name. Amen.

∼

---

2. *Strong's Greek: 5590. ψυχή (psuchē) -- breath, the soul.* (n.d.). https://biblehub.com/greek/5590.htm

5

THE SIGNIFICANCE IN THE MENIAL TASKS OF LIFE

"I can do all things through Christ who strengthens me."
(Philippians 4:13)

"Rejoice in the Lord alway, again I say rejoice."
(Philippians 4:4)

~

The Bible contains well-known names such as David, Esther, Daniel, and Moses. However, in Philippians 2, we encounter a relatively unknown man named Epaphroditus. There are no recorded sermons preached by him. We are never told of him performing a miracle. Yet, he gets his name in the Word of God!

Epaphroditus is introduced to us simply because he performed the role of an ancient mail courier. He brought a gift from the church at Philippi to the apostle Paul, who was in prison in Rome. On his return, he carried a letter from Paul back to the Philippian church, which we know as the Book of Philippians.

Epaphroditus' faithfulness in this menial role brought us verses we often quote, like "I can do all things through Christ who strengthens me." (Philippians 4:13) and "Rejoice in the Lord alway, again I say rejoice." (Philippians 4:4)

We are all called to menial tasks every day. We may feel they are unnoticed and unimportant and wonder if our life impacts anyone. However, like Epaphroditus, your faithfulness in these tasks could be the very thing that blesses others. Who knows? One day, someone may even read about you as the one who carried God's message to your generation.

Prayer

Lord, I thank You for the gift of ordinary days and the countless opportunities they bring to serve You. Help me to recognize the importance of being faithful in the mundane tasks of life, knowing that You see and value my diligence and dedication. May I find joy and purpose in every small act of faithfulness, trusting that You are using them to shape me and advance Your kingdom. Amen.

6

THE DIVINE DUMPSTER-DIVER

"He lifts the poor from the dust, the needy from the garbage dump."
(1 Samuel 2:8)

My garbage bin has become a source of worship. Every Wednesday evening, I roll the garbage bin to the road so that the sanitation workers can drive by on Thursday morning and take away the collection of discarded items, rubbish, and things that we no longer want.

I ran across a fantastic verse in 1 Samuel, where Hannah, after many years of sorrow because she could not have children, finally gave birth to the eventual prophet, Samuel. When she did, she burst forth in song. In one verse of her song she sang, "He lifts the poor from the dust," and get this, "the needy from the garbage dump." (1 Samuel 2:8)

No disrespect intended, but I love the thought that God, the God who created the universe, the God who created everything, is a Divine dumpster diver. He dives into the garbage dump of life for you and me. The world would willingly and easily discard us because of our failures and struggles. But when everyone else would discard us and leave us in the garbage dump, like a prodigal in the pigpen with the muck and the mire of life, the Father ran down the road of our country to rescue us from the garbage of our lives.

So the next time you're pushing your garbage to the road, let me encourage you to let it be a cue to worship God's amazing love and willingness to rescue you in this life.

Prayer

Heavenly Father, I come before You with a heart full of gratitude, thanking You for rescuing me from the garbage of my sins. Your mercy and grace have lifted me from the depths of despair and given me a new life in Your love. I am forever grateful for Your forgiveness and the hope You have restored in me. Amen.

7
THE SOUND OF SILENCE

"Be still, and know that I am God"
(Psalm 46:10)

The anechoic chamber at Orfield Laboratories in Minnesota is the quietest place on earth, with background noise measured at -9.4 dBA. Steven Orfield, the lab's founder, says that the ears adapt to the chamber's dark, absolute quiet, leading to heightened internal awareness. You become the only sound you hear. You will hear the beating of your heart and the gurgling of your stomach. This extreme quiet has both intrigued and challenged those who have experienced it. So profound is the silence that the longest stay recorded is 45 minutes.[1]

When we take the time to be still, who knows what we might hear? Perhaps that is why, in the Bible, people often view

---

1. Galloway, L. (February 24, 2022). *The quietest place on Earth*. BBC.com. https://www.bbc.com/travel/article/20121022-the-quietest-place-on-earth

moments of silence and reflection as opportunities to discover God. "Be still, and know that I am God." (Psalm 46:10) Silence provides an opportunity to listen more intently and explore God's presence. In a world that is constantly screaming for our attention, it is imperative that we intentionally take time to be quiet, focus on God, and allow His Spirit to stir the innermost parts of our being.

But like the quietness of the anechoic chamber, sitting in silence to focus on God's Spirit, whispering can be daunting at first. According to Psalms 46:10, it is the way we experience the intimacy of His presence.

∽

Prayer

Lord, it is in the quietness of Your presence that I often recognize You are God. In those moments, teach me to rest in Your Spirit. In the noise of my life, quiet my heart and my mind, enabling me to be strengthened, comforted, and assured by the presence of Your Spirit. Amen

∽

8
JUST ADD AN EGG

"And we sent Timothy to visit you. He is our brother and God's co-worker in proclaiming the Good News of Christ. We sent him to strengthen you, to encourage you in your faith."
(1 Thessalonians 3:2)

When the Betty Crocker cake mixes were first introduced in the 1950s, General Mills wanted to make life simpler and easier for homemakers. However, their product was a flop. They discovered homemakers felt guilty because they were not putting enough personal effort into making the cakes. Their solution? They removed eggs from the ingredients and put the words "Add An Egg" on the front of the box. Sales skyrocketed.[1]

God can do anything and everything. And the reality is, He doesn't need our help. But amazingly, He invites us to be co-

---

1. Moritz, Janet A. (2021) *"The Sweet History of Boxed Cake Mix."* Allrecipes/com. https://www.allrecipes.com/article/history-of-boxed-cake-mix/.

laborers in His work. Our contributions, though small compared to His, allow us to participate in something with eternal significance.

In 1 Thessalonians 3:2, Paul describes Timothy as "God's co-worker in proclaiming the Good News of Jesus Christ." In everything you do today, even those things that are difficult or mundane, remember you are working along with God. That's quite a partnership.

∼

Prayer

Heavenly Father, I want to say thank You for the incredible opportunity to be a part of Your work. Please let me be a co-worker with You in building Your kingdom. Use me in any way You see fit, and help me stay open, willing, and ready to serve alongside You. Amen.

∼

❧ 9 ☙
THE PLACEMENT OF THE COMMA

"When the enemy shall come in, like a flood the Spirit of the Lord shall lift up a standard against him."
(Isaiah 59:19 KJV)

The placement of the comma in Isaiah 59:19 has sparked debate among Bible scholars. Since the original Hebrew text lacks punctuation, translators must decide where to place it based on their interpretation.

The debate surrounds the placement of the comma in one of two ways:

1. "When the enemy shall come in like a flood, the Spirit of the Lord shall lift up a standard against him."

2. "When the enemy shall come in, like a flood the Spirit of the Lord shall lift up a standard against him."

Interpreting this passage hinges on whether "like a flood"

describes the enemy's attack or the Lord's response. Some scholars argue that "like a flood" should represent the overwhelming power of the Lord's response rather than the manner of the enemy's coming.

I find both interpretations encouraging. They describe the Lord responding powerfully to protect His people when the enemy comes against us. Seeing the Lord flooding His presence into every difficult situation is an exceptional word-picture. Wherever the comma falls, may we remember God is with us when the enemy comes against us.

∼

Prayer

Jesus, I thank You for always being with me, especially when the enemy comes against me. Your presence and strength are my refuge and my defense. I praise You for standing by my side and giving me the courage to face any challenge. Amen.

∼

10
EATING AT THE KING'S TABLE

"And Mephibosheth, who was crippled in both feet, lived in Jerusalem and ate regularly at the king's table."
(2 Samuel 9:13)

"Come to Me, all who labor and are heavy laden, and I will give you rest"
(Matthew 11:28)

In 2 Samuel 9:13, there is a beautiful depiction of grace and acceptance as Mephibosheth, despite his lameness, eats at King David's table, much like one of the king's own sons. "And Mephibosheth, who was crippled in both feet, lived in Jerusalem and ate regularly at the king's table." (NLT)

The king gives Mephibosheth, who represents us with our imperfections and brokenness, a place of honor and fellowship at his table.

This story resonates deeply with my story. Just as David

invited Mephibosheth, God extended an invitation to me (and all of us) through Jesus Christ. It doesn't matter how broken we feel or how deep our struggles are; His table is a place where we find acceptance and belonging.

Jesus said, "Come to Me, all who labor and are heavy laden, and I will give you rest" (Matthew 11:28). At God's table, the grace of Christ embraces and restores us, not defining us by our shortcomings. This is the essence of God's unending love and mercy towards us.

∼

Prayer

Father, I just want to thank You for Your amazing grace in allowing me to feast at Your table. Your love and mercy are beyond what I can comprehend, and I'm so grateful for the chance to be in Your presence. Thank You for welcoming me with open arms and filling my life with Your goodness. Amen.

∼

11
WHAT A POWERFUL NAME IT IS

"On his robe at his thigh was written this title: King of all kings and Lord of all Lords."
(Revelation 19:16)

Did you know that the bone in your thigh, the femur, can hold up to 30 times your body weight, close to 6,000 pounds?[1]

Stay with me on this. John, in his Revelation, said that he saw heaven open and One standing there whose "eyes were like flames of fire, and on his head were many crowns" (Revelation 19:12 NLT). "He wore a robe dipped in blood, and his title was the Word of God." (Revelation 19:13) And get this! "On his robe at HIS THIGH was written this title: King of all kings and Lord of all Lords." (Revelation 19:16)

I don't think the King's name, inscribed on the sash at His

---

1. Interesting Facts. *Your femur can support 30 times the weight of your body.* https://www.interestingfacts.com/fact/655cfa5c78a86d8b8059f907

thigh, is a coincidence. He has His mighty name inscribed on the sash at His thigh. Remember, the next time you are struggling and wondering if He can carry you.

> *You have no rival*
> *You have no equal*
> *Now and forever God You reign*
> *Yours is the kingdom*
> *Yours is the glory*
> *Yours is the Name above all names.*
> *What a powerful Name it is - the Name of Jesus.*[2]

∼

Prayer

Jesus, I just want to lift up Your powerful name in worship and praise. Your name is above all names, full of strength and majesty, and it brings hope and peace to my heart. Thank You for the power and protection Your name provides; I am in awe of Your greatness. Amen.

∼

---

2. Fielding, Ben and Ligertwood, Brooke. (2017) *What A Beautiful Name.* Hillsong Publishing, Hillsong Music Publishing Australia

12
SIGNIFICANT WORK ISN'T ALWAYS GLAMOROUS

"So the Jewish elders continued their work, and they were greatly encouraged by the preaching of the prophets Haggai and Zechariah son of Iddo. The Temple was finally finished, as had been commanded by the God of Israel and decreed by Cyrus, Darius, and Artaxerxes, the kings of Persia. The Temple was completed on March 12, during the sixth year of King Darius's reign."
(Ezra 6:14)

In the story of Israel's return from exile, Ezra 6:14 records Zerubbabel's rebuilding of the temple. The temple's reconstruction restored the spiritual center of Israel with a grand celebration. What an honor! To build a place that represented the abiding presence of God on earth.

However, they did not rebuild the wall to protect the temple from invaders. 70 years later, Nehemiah undertook the critical yet less glamorous task of rebuilding Jerusalem's wall. Most would agree that wall-building is not nearly as attention-getting as temple-building.

Like Nehemiah, you may not have a glamorous role that attracts attention. However, the lesson of Nehemiah is that not all SIGNIFICANT work is GLAMOROUS. Most of us are called to tasks that might lack outward glory, but they are crucial in God's plan.

Oh, yes! Don't forget that Nehemiah had an entire book in the Old Testament named after him, and we often turn to Nehemiah to teach timeless leadership principles. How's that for significance?

∽

Prayer
I ask for Your help in staying faithful, even in the little, insignificant tasks. Sometimes, it's hard to see the purpose in the small stuff, but I know You value every bit of it. Give me the strength and dedication to do everything with a willing heart for Your glory. Amen.

∽

13
DO NOT FEAR BAD NEWS

"They do not fear bad news; they confidently trust the Lord to care for them. They are confident and fearless and can face their foes triumphantly."
(Psalms 112:7-8)

Wouldn't it be wonderful if we all lived in Garrison Keillor's mythical city of Lake Wobegon from his radio program, "A Prairie Home Companion," which aired on NPR from 1974 through 2016? Keillor usually began his stories with, "Well, it's been a quiet week in Lake Wobegon, Minnesota, my hometown." He would close the monologue with, "That's the news from Lake Wobegon, where all the women are strong, all the men are good-looking, and all the children are above average."

Of course, Lake Wobegon is fictional. Most of us seldom have a quiet week. Life isn't without bad news. That's why I love Psalm 112.

My favorite verses are 7 and 8, "They do not fear bad news; they confidently trust the Lord to care for them. They are confident and fearless and can face their foes triumphantly." There is "bad news," and we must "face [our] foes".

However, we do not fear the bad news, and we are confident and fearless as we face our foes triumphantly. Why? Because "we confidently trust the Lord to care for [us]." So, when it isn't a quiet week in your hometown, and you are facing foes, remember to trust Him, who cares for you.

"I sought the Lord, and He heard, and He answered! That's why I trust him! That's why I trust Him!"[1]

∽

Prayer

Lord, I ask for the ability to trust You completely, even when there's so much happening in the world that could cause fear. Help me lean on Your promises and find peace in Your presence. Give me the courage to face uncertainty with faith, knowing You are always in control. Amen.

∽

---

1. Lake, Brandon, Brown, Christopher Joel, Wong, Mitch, Furtick, Steve. (2023). *Trust In God.* Essential Music Publishing, Integrity Music

14
HIS WORD WILL NOT RETURN EMPTY

"The rain and snow come down from the heavens and stay on the ground to water the earth. They cause the grain to grow, producing seed for the farmer and bread for the hungry. It is the same with my word. I send it out, and it always produces fruit. It will accomplish all I want it to, and it will prosper everywhere I send it."
(Isaiah 55:10-11)

"Be sure of this: I am with you always, even to the end of the age."
(Matthew 28:20)

When you were in elementary school, you probably learned about the process of rain and evaporation. In short, it rains; the rain nourishes the earth; the rain evaporates to form clouds that create rain again. Because of this cycle, some scientists say we drink the same rain the dinosaurs drank.[1]

---

1. *Do we drink water from dinosaur days?* (November 26, 2018). Ask Dr. Universe,

Interestingly, God uses the same analogy to describe the impact of His Word on the affairs of earth. Isaiah 55:10-11, "As the rain and the snow come down from heaven, and do not return to it without watering the earth… so is my word that goes out from my mouth: It will not return to me empty, but will accomplish what I desire."

Think about it! The same Word spoken to Abraham, the same Word spoken to Moses, the same word spoken to Simon Peter, is the same Word spoken to you. And the promise is, "It will not return…empty, but will accomplish what [He] desires!"

Let me leave you with just one shower of blessing today. This promise spoken to the original apostles is spoken to you. "Be sure of this: I am with you always, even to the end of the age." (Matthew 28:20)

∽

Prayer

Father, I declare my trust in the power of Your Word. No matter what's going on around me, I know that Your promises are true and Your Word is unshakable. Help me to stand firm in my faith, finding strength and guidance in Your powerful truth. Amen.

∽

Washington State University. https://askdruniverse.wsu.edu/2016/04/10/drink-water-dinosaur-days/

15
LONG OF NOSE

"The Lord passed in front of Moses, calling out, "Yahweh! The Lord! The God of compassion and mercy! I am slow to anger and filled with unfailing love and faithfulness."
(Exodus 34:6)

At 6'6", I'm accustomed to the frequent exclamations of, "Wow! You're tall!" that greet me when I meet people. While I'm tempted to respond with a touch of sarcasm—"Thank you for telling me, I had no idea!"—I usually just offer a smile in return. But you know what's funny? I often describe myself with that same feature. I often default to describing myself as "tall".

That reminds me of a powerful moment from the Bible, where God introduces Himself to Moses not by His might or splendor but with a deeply personal self-description. In Exodus 34:6, we read, "Yahweh! The Lord! The God of compassion and mercy! I am slow to anger and filled with unfailing love and faithfulness."

In this passage, the Hebrew phrase "trek apayim" describes "slow to anger." It literally means "long of nose". But rather than referring to physical traits, this expression signifies patience, such as taking a long, deep breath to temper frustration with calmness.[1]

Let's not overlook the beauty of the imagery in this Divine self-declaration: God leads with compassion and mercy, qualities that are embodied in His "unfailing love and faithfulness." Personally, I find great solace in looking up to a Father who is metaphorically "long of nose."

∽

Prayer

Holy Spirit, I ask for the fruit of the Spirit to fill my heart with patience and mercy in my relationships. Help me show love and understanding, even when it's hard. Let Your Spirit guide me in treating others with the same grace and kindness You've shown me. Amen.

∽

---

1. *Exodus 34:6 Hebrew Text analysis*. (n.d.). https://biblehub.com/text/exodus/34-6.htm

16
WHAT CAUSES GOD TO REJOICE

"Do not despise these small beginnings, for the Lord rejoices to see the work begin."
(Zechariah 4:10)

In our culture, we applaud those who accomplish great things. They speak at huge conferences, appear on podcasts, and climb best-seller book lists. And there is nothing wrong with that. We should applaud the great things God has done in the lives and ministries of others.

But in our applause for those who have completed great things, let's never forget that God gets super excited about those who BEGIN SMALL THINGS (yes, I know in social media vernacular I'm shouting…it's on purpose)!

"Do not despise these small beginnings, for the Lord rejoices to see the work begin." (Zechariah 4:10)

I love this quote from Jon Chasteen,

> *"The real test of our character...is whether we are willing to plant seeds that will grow into trees, even though we may never sit under the shade of or pick fruit from their branches."[1]*

Rest assured, what you are doing today may never get you on a podcast, at a large conference, or on a best-seller list, but if you are faithfully doing what He has called you to do, God is celebrating with you!

Prayer

Heavenly Father, help me to trust in Your plan and do my part with a willing heart, even when I can't see the results. Give me the patience and perseverance to sow seeds for future generations, knowing that You will bring the growth in Your perfect time. Amen.

---

1. Chasteen, J. (2024). *Releader: How to Fix What You Didn't Break*, p. 154. XLeadership:Southlake, TX

17
GOD NOTICES THE DETAILS

"The very hairs on your head are all numbered."
(Luke 12:7)

∼

1 Kings 7 recounts King Solomon's construction of the grand temple in Jerusalem. He employed a skilled artisan, Huram, who built massive pillars 37 1/2 feet tall and 18 feet in circumference. Though probably unnoticed by most, the Bible highlights, *"The capitals on the two pillars had 200 pomegranates in two rows around them"* (1 Kings 7:20).

The pomegranates at the top of the pillars, though seemingly insignificant and probably unseen by most, held great significance for Huram. They were a testament to his craftsmanship and attention to detail. While most people would have overlooked them, God and Huram recognized and appreciated the intricate details at the top of the columns.

God's understanding of the significance of the little things in our lives, even those that may seem unimportant to others, is a testament to His deep love and care for us. If it matters to us, it matters to Him, underscoring the personal connection we have with our Creator.

Just as God paid attention to the details of the pomegranates at the top of the pillars in the temple, He is also attentive to the seemingly insignificant details of our lives. How insignificant? *"The very hairs on your head are all numbered."*

∼

Prayer

Jesus, I thank You for Your deep love and care for every detail of my life. Your attentiveness to my joys, sorrows, and needs reassures me of Your constant presence and compassion. May I always trust in Your tender care, knowing that nothing is too insignificant for Your loving concern. Amen.

∼

18

GOD IS SPEAKING

"Your own ears will hear Him. Right behind you a voice will say, 'This is the way you should go,' whether to the right or to the left"
(Isaiah 30:21)

Caroll Spinney, who was cast to play and voice a new muppet named Oscar the Grouch on Sesame Street, struggled with finding the right voice that fit the character's grumpy nature, one that distinct from other Muppet voices. Despite his efforts in experimenting with different voices, none seemed satisfactory. Then he encountered a taxi driver, who embodied the exact vocal quality he was looking for. When Spinney got in his taxi, the driver asked, "Where to, Mac?"[1]

I often hear Christians say things like "If I could just hear the Lord...." Our attempt to follow Him is made more difficult when

---

1. Spinney, C., & Milligan, J. (2007). *The wisdom of Big Bird (and the dark genius of Oscar The Grouch): Lessons from a Life in Feathers*, pp 50-51. Villard.

we feel as though He isn't speaking to us. But it may surprise you to discover the many places where you can hear the voice of God speaking into your life if you purposely live each day to listen carefully to His voice. "Your own ears will hear Him. Right behind you a voice will say, 'This is the way you should go,' whether to the right or to the left." (Isaiah 30:21)

Make no mistake. God is speaking. It is His desire to guide and direct us in the everyday episodes of our lives. Perhaps today, in someone as unexpected as a grumpy taxi driver or in a place as unpredictable as heavy traffic, we can hear Him.

∼

Prayer

God, we humbly ask that You help us hear Your voice amidst the noise and distractions of our daily lives. Open our hearts and minds to Your guidance, so we may discern Your will and follow Your path with faith and clarity. May Your gentle whisper lead us closer to You, filling us with wisdom and peace. Amen.

∼

19
MELTING MY FEARS

"Be humble, thinking of others as better than yourselves."
(Philippians 2:3)

One of the pivotal scenes in the cinema classic, "The Wizard of Oz," occurs toward the end when the Wicked Witch of the West sets the Scarecrow on fire. Dorothy, terrified of the Witch (which in reality is a dream where the witch represents a grumpy spinster Dorothy had encountered in real life), grabs a bucket of water and throws it on the Scarecrow to douse the fire. In doing so, she also drenches the Witch, and everyone discovers that the water destroys the villain. (Can't you hear her? "I'm melting! I'm melting!")

Author Seth Godin writes, "[Dorothy] finds the courage to overcome her fear when she's generously supporting a friend."[1]

---

1. Godin, Seth. (April 1, 2024). *Generosity and fear*. Seth's Blog. https://seths.blog/2024/04/generosity-and-fear/

Having a strong intent to serve minimizes our fears.

Centuries before Dorothy's example, the Apostle Paul wrote, "Be humble, thinking of others as better than yourselves." (Philippians 2:3)

I know from my own experiences that when I think of others, my fears melt.

∽

Prayer

God, I want to ask for the faith and courage to serve others, knowing that it will melt away my fears. Help me focus on helping those around me, trusting that in giving of myself, You'll calm my anxieties. Fill me with Your love and strength so that I can make a difference in the lives of others without fear. Amen.

∽

20

SPEAKING THE LANGUAGE

"And everyone present was filled with the Holy Spirit and began speaking in other languages, as the Holy Spirit gave them this ability."
(Acts 2:4)

"They were completely amazed. "How can this be?" they exclaimed. "These people are all from Galilee, and yet we hear them speaking in our own native languages!"
(Acts 2:7-8)

Acts 2:4 reads, "And everyone present was filled with the Holy Spirit and began speaking in other languages, as the Holy Spirit gave them this ability."

As this outpouring occurred, people from other provinces and nations gathered in Jerusalem for Pentecost and were attracted to the upper room. Verses 7 and 8 describe their reaction. "They were completely amazed. "How can this be?"

they exclaimed. "These people are all from Galilee, and yet we hear them speaking in our own native languages!"

"Speaking in our own native languages." While this refers to their native tongues and dialects, I think it is relevant to us today. Shouldn't those around us hear us speaking their language?

Shouldn't we speak the language of the caregiver who is by the bed of an aging parent? How about the language of the business executive who is overwhelmed with the demands of balancing income, expenses, and human resources? Who will speak the language of the teens trying to find themselves in a world constantly telling them who they should be? Or the language of a couple trying to make ends meet, crunched by time expectations from work, children, and church?

I pray my Pentecost experience will speak the language of those I encounter daily.

Prayer

Holy Spirit, I thank You for Your presence in my life. I am grateful for the wonderful gifts You give us. I ask for Your wisdom in allowing your presence in my life to impact those I come in contact with each day. May the love of God speak through my life to encourage those who need to hear from You. Amen.

21
LABELS

"His mother was Bathsheba, the widow of Uriah"
(Matthew 1:6, KJV)

"But God removed Saul and replaced him with David, a man about whom God said, 'I have found David son of Jesse, a man after my own heart. He will do everything I want him to do.'"
(Acts 13:22)

It was just a parenthetical statement found in Jesus' genealogy concerning his son, Solomon. But for King David, the father of Solomon, it was so much more. It was...a label. "His mother was Bathsheba, the widow of Uriah" (Matthew 1:6).

Twenty-eight generations had passed from David's adulterous sin with Bathsheba and the murder of her husband, Uriah. But even in the genealogy, the label stuck.

People can do that to us. In others' eyes, our past failures, mistakes, and mess-ups can label us for life. But God did not do that to David. While the genealogist may have reminded us that Solomon was the son of Bathsheba, the widow of Uriah, a moment of one of David's most significant failures, God re-labeled David as "a man after my own heart" (Acts 13:22).

That is the work of redemption! That is why His grace is amazing, and His love is marvelous!

∼

Prayer

Heavenly Father, I thank You for your amazing grace and love. Thank You that, regardless of my past, You have given me a new start and a new life. Help me to always cherish the sacrifice You gave so that I could be made new.

∼

22
HOW I FIGHT MY BATTLES

"After the death of Joshua, the Israelites asked the Lord, "Which tribe should go first to attack the Canaanites?" The Lord answered, "Judah, for I have given them victory over the land."
(*Judges 1:1-2*)

Judges 1:1-2 is a pivotal moment where the Israelites seek God's guidance after Joshua's passing. "After the death of Joshua, the Israelites asked the Lord, "Which tribe should go first to attack the Canaanites?"

The Lord's response is specific and profound: "The Lord answered, 'Judah, for I have given them victory over the land.'" This isn't just a strategic military move; it's a spiritual declaration. The name "Judah" in Hebrew means "praise", from the root *yadah*.[1] This choice by God underscores a timeless truth: victory always begins with praise.

---

1. Strong's H3063 - *Yehudah*. Bible Hub, https://biblehub.com/hebrew/3063.htm.

Verse 3 says, "The men of Judah said to their relatives from the tribe of Simeon, Join with us to fight against the Canaanites living in the territory allotted to us." Interestingly, the Hebrew word "Simeon" means "God has heard", from the root *Shim`on*.[2] Don't miss the impact of that truth. When we praise Him, God hears, and, like Simeon with Judah, He fights for us!

This story isn't just about conquest; it's a testament to the power of praise and worship during our battles. "This is how I fight my battles!"

Prayer

Heavenly Father, often in the heat of battles, I become focused on requests for deliverance. But I know you inhabit the praises of Your people. So today, even during my struggles, I give You praise, and I worship You because You are God, and You are worthy of my praise.

---

2. Strong's H8095 - *Shim'on*. Bible Hub. https://biblehub.com/hebrew/8095.htm.

23
A HAPPY HEART

"A glad heart makes a happy face; a broken heart crushes the spirit. A cheerful heart is good medicine."
(Proverbs 15:13, 17:22)

A study from Brazil highlights the cardiovascular benefits of laughter therapy, demonstrating that even a tiny giggle can expand cardiac tissue and enhance oxygen flow in the body, benefiting heart health.[1]

The study involved 26 adults, with an average age of 64, with coronary artery disease. For three months, researchers divided the participants into two groups: one group watched comedy programs, and the other group viewed serious documentaries. Those who watched comedies experienced a 10% increase in

---

1. Steinberg, Brooke. (August 28, 2023) *"Laughter Can Heal a Broken Heart, Literally: Cardiac Health Study."* New York Post. https://nypost.com/2023/08/28/laughter-can-heal-a-broken-heart-literally-cardiac-health-study/.

their heart's oxygen pumping capacity. Laughter releases endorphins, maintaining healthy blood pressure and reducing heart strain by keeping stress hormones low.

The study recommends engaging in laughter-inducing activities at least twice weekly to enhance happiness and reduce the risk of heart attack and stroke.

Isn't it amazing how, when science moves beyond theory, it verifies the teachings of the Scriptures? "A glad heart makes a happy face; a broken heart crushes the spirit. A cheerful heart is good medicine." (Proverbs 15:13, 17:22) So, improve your health today. Laugh a little.

∽

Prayer

Holy Spirit, I know that one evidence of Your fruit in my life is joy. I rejoice today because the joy of the Lord is my strength. I ask you to always work within the depths of my spirit to enable me to rejoice in the Lord, always.

∽

24
FAITHFUL

"Well done, My good and FAITHFUL servant"
(Matt. 25:21)

".. the righteous will live by their faithfulness to God."
(Habakkuk 2:4)

A few years ago, I was looking through a scrapbook from when I was younger. Tucked among articles from my hometown newspaper about basketball games I participated in was a copy of something I'm sure most people my age did not keep...the report of my ACT scores from the only time I took the test for college entrance.

When you registered to take the test, you listed your top three fields of study in college. My number 1 choice was baffling. Oceanography! Now understand, I grew up in Oklahoma and had never seen an ocean at the time. My only explanation is that I must have watched a documentary about Jacque Cousteau (if you're under 50, Google it). I didn't pursue that major (the college I attended didn't offer it).

Children often express extraordinary ambitions when asked, "What do you want to be when you grow up?" Doctor. Professional Athlete. Superhero. I do not believe I have ever heard a child respond this way: "Faithful."

And yet, Jesus tells us that when we get to heaven, if we've lived a life that pleases him, He will say, *"Well done, My good and FAITHFUL servant" (Matt. 25:21).* He will only honor us if we have the descriptors of "good" and "faithful". Faithfulness requires intentionality.

You don't just drift into faithfulness. You make a choice. *".. the righteous will live by their faithfulness to God."* So, what do you want to be when you grow up? I hope your answer is "faithful".

∼

Prayer

Jesus, I seek Your strength and guidance to remain faithful in all that I do. Help me stay committed and diligent, even in the smallest tasks, knowing that my faithfulness brings glory to Your name. Fill my heart with Your steadfast love and empower me to serve You with unwavering devotion every day. Amen.

∼

25
YOU JUST NEVER KNOW

"So, my dear brothers and sisters, be strong and immovable. Always work enthusiastically for the Lord, for you know that nothing you do for the Lord is ever useless."
(1 Corinthians 15:58)

∽

In 1912, Dr. William Leslie, a medical missionary, ventured to the Democratic Republic of the Congo, dedicating 17 years to tribal communities in a remote corner. He returned to the U.S. disheartened, feeling his efforts to spread Christianity had failed.

However, in 2010, Eric Ramsey and Tom Cox World Ministries discovered Leslie's unforeseen legacy: a vibrant network of churches thriving in the jungle near Vanga. Contrary to Leslie's belief, his mission had flourished, resulting in a 1,000-seat stone cathedral, many village churches, and a tradition of gospel choirs and musical exchanges between villages. Leslie also introduced the first structured education system, leaving a profound spiritual and cultural impact.[1]

You just never know! And you may never know...this side of heaven. But know this... what you do makes a difference! "So, my dear brothers and sisters, be strong and immovable. Always work enthusiastically for the Lord, for you know that nothing you do for the Lord is ever useless." (1 Corinthians 15:58)

Prayer

Heavenly Father, sometimes it seems my labors are in vain. There are moments when I do not see fruit from what I am doing for you. I ask that the Holy Spirit always remind me that nothing I do for You is ever useless. You will produce a harvest in due season. Amen.

---

1. Ellis, Mark. (May 1, 2014) *"Missionary Died Thinking He Was a Failure; 84 Years Later, Thriving Churches Found Hidden in the Jungle."* God Reports. https://www.godreports.com/2014/05/missionary-died-thinking-he-was-a-failure-84-years-later-thriving-churches-found-hidden-in-the-jungle/.

26

SEEN IN THE SHADOWS

"Even the darkness will not be dark to You; the night will shine like the day, for darkness is as light to You."
(Psalm 139:12, NIV)

Novelist Carlos Ruiz Zalón wrote in "The Shadow of the Wind", "Some things can only be seen in the shadows."[1]

Psalm 139:12 (NIV) declares, "Even the darkness will not be dark to You; the night will shine like the day, for darkness is as light to You." The Hebrew term 'choshek' in this verse signifies not just darkness, but also mystery, obscurity, and a lack of understanding.[2]

We all have events in our lives that cast a shadow over our ability to comprehend why they are happening. In these

---

1. Zafón, Carlos Ruiz. (2004). *The Shadow of the Wind.* New York: Penguin Press
2. Strong's H2822 - *"Choshek."* Bible Hub. https://biblehub.com/hebrew/2822.htm.

moments of 'chosek,' our faith is not just tested but refined, and our reliance on God grows, becoming a beacon of hope in the darkness.

Shadows are often opportunities for spiritual growth and deeper communion with God. In your own "choshek", remember for there to be a shadow, there must be a light.

∽

Prayer

Father, I know that life will not always be cheerful and bright. Dark days will come my way. Help me have the faith to see Your hand working in those moments. Give me the grace to trust Your presence will be with me and that Your light will shine on me, giving me direction and guidance. Amen

∽

27

THE LORD WILL HELP US

"Let's go across to the outpost of those pagans," Jonathan said to his armor bearer. "Perhaps the Lord will help us, for nothing can hinder the Lord. He can win a battle whether He has many warriors or only a few!"
(1 Samuel 14:6)

One of my favorite stories in the Old Testament is the account of Jonathan and his armor-bearer confronting overwhelming odds. In 1 Samuel 14:1-7, Jonathan proposed a daring attack on the Philistine garrison, demonstrating his faith and courage. They plan to reveal themselves to the Philistines, interpreting the enemies' response as a sign from God on whether to attack.

"Let's go across to the outpost of those pagans," Jonathan said to his armor bearer. "Perhaps the Lord will help us, for nothing can hinder the Lord. He can win a battle whether He has many warriors or only a few!" (1 Samuel 14:6)

I love what Christine Caine writes in "You're Not Finished Yet":

"I think one of the greatest keys to long-term endurance is to be willing to live in the 'perhaps' realm. If we wait for sixteen confirmations from God and three visitations from angels dancing on our beds before we do anything, we will never do anything. The life of faith is a life of risks." [1]

May we live in the "perhaps" realm. Who knows, but if today, "the Lord will help us!"

∽

Prayer

I ask for the courage to live a life of risks, fully trusting You to help me along the way. Help me step out in faith, knowing that You are always with me and will guide my every move. Let my trust in You be stronger than my fears, so I can live boldly for Your glory. Amen.

∽

---

1. Caine, Christine. (2021) *You're Not Finished Yet*, p. 97. Grand Rapids: Zondervan

28
YOUR FLAWS DON'T DISQUALIFY YOU

"And the God of all grace, who called you to his eternal glory in Christ, after you have suffered a little while, will himself restore you and make you strong, firm and steadfast."
(1 Peter 5:10 NIV).

I realize I'm late to the party. Arts and crafts people already know this. But as an average non-creative, I recently discovered an ancient Japanese craft called kintsugi. Nicole Silva of NBCnews.com says,

> "Kintsugi is the Japanese art of putting broken pottery pieces back together with gold — built on the idea that in embracing flaws and imperfections, you can create an even stronger, more beautiful piece of art. Every break is unique and instead of repairing an item like new, the

400-year-old technique actually highlights the 'scars' as a part of the design."[1]

The ancient craft of *kintsugi* is more ancient than that. God has been practicing it since the Garden of Eden. "And the God of all grace, who called you to his eternal glory in Christ, after you have suffered a little while, will himself restore you and make you strong, firm and steadfast." (1 Peter 5:10).

Something beautiful, Something good.
All my confusion, He understood.
All I had to offer Him was brokenness and strife
But He made something beautiful of my life.[2]

Your flaws don't disqualify you. In the Master Potter's hands, you more beautiful and stronger than ever.

∼

Prayer
Jesus, I thank You for restoring me when I was broken. Help me remember that no matter how broken I feel, Your power to heal and transform is greater. Let my life be a testimony of Your amazing grace and ability to use even the most broken vessels for Your glory. Amen.

∼

---

1. Silva, Nicole. (2018) *"How the Japanese Art Technique 'Kintsugi' Can Help You Be More Resilient."* NBCnews.com. https://www.nbcnews.com/better/health/how-japanese-art-technique-kintsugi-can-help-you-be-more-ncna866471.
2. Gaither, Bill, and Gloria Gaither. (1971) *Something Beautiful*. Nashville: Gaither Music.

29
SEEING THROUGH THE STRUGGLES

"Because of the joy awaiting Him, He endured the cross, disregarding its shame."
(Hebrews 12:2)

A few decades ago, "Magic Eye" images were trendy. You would look at the picture a certain way, and a 3D object would "magically" pop out of it. Unfortunately, I could never master the technique or see what others saw.

Until...one day, a student at Hamilton Heights said, "Mr. Stone, I'm going to help you." He held the picture a few feet away and told me to look through it to try to see his stomach. As I began focusing "through the picture," a giraffe popped out of the conglomeration, floating magically in front of the abstract background. By "looking through" the obvious, I could see the ultimate.

Listen to the words of Hebrews 12:2, "Because of the joy awaiting Him, He endured the cross, disregarding its shame."

Can you see it? Behind the cross, the shame, the pain, was the "joy awaiting Him." Jesus looked through the cross and saw the joy.

And it is there for you as well. When your heart is crushed, when your cross seems too heavy to bear, have faith. Look beyond the pain, and see the joy awaiting those who remain faithful. This faith, this belief, has the power to transform your struggles into victories.

~

Prayer

Father, help me see through my struggles and glimpse the victory on the other side. Help me trust in Your strength and hold on to the hope You provide, even when times are tough. Let me keep my eyes on the victory You've promised, knowing that You are with me every step of the way. Amen.

~

30

THEY MAKE ME SMELL GOOD

"Now He uses us to spread the knowledge of Christ everywhere, like a sweet perfume."
(2 Corinthians 2:14)

∽

According to zoologists, an elephant's trunk contains more muscles (40,000) than the entire human body (650).[1] It can also smell water sources 12 miles away![2]

The elephant's sense of smell reminds me of a distinguished couple who attended a church I pastored. They always dressed

---

1. BBC. (n.d.) *"10 Surprising Things About Elephants."* BBC.com bbc.co.uk. https://www.bbc.co.uk/programmes/articles/4ZNLJ9Nyrjlz3snl5wvWHmT/10-surprising-things-about-elephants#:-:text=An%20elephant's%20trunk%20contains%20over,which%20contains%20only%20639%20muscles.
2. SeaWorld. (n.d.) *"Elephants: Characteristics."* Seaworld.org. https://seaworld.org/animals/all-about/elephants/characteristics/#:-:text=Through%20this%20process%2C%20elephants%20are,legs%20and%20extending%20their%20trunk.

eloquently, and because of their cologne and perfume, they always smelled wonderful.

One day, as they entered our church lobby, I was standing with several other people, greeting and talking, when they both bent over and hugged a five or six-year-old boy. As they walked away, the little boy looked at me and said, "I like them. They make me smell good!"

Paul wrote to the Corinthians, "Now He uses us to spread the knowledge of Christ everywhere, like a sweet perfume." (2 Corinthians 2:14). May my life have such a sweet aroma that the people I encounter each day "smell good" because of our encounter.

Prayer

Holy Spirit, anoint me to be a sweet aroma to the Father in everything I do. Help me to live a life that is pleasing and fragrant to Him, showing love and kindness to everyone around me. Let my actions and words reflect His goodness and bring joy to His heart. Amen.

31
YOU DRIFT WHERE YOU LOOK

"Let your eyes look straight ahead; fix your gaze directly before you."
(Proverbs 4:25 NIV)

When I turned 15, I was legally required to take a Driver's Education class to get my Learner's Permit and eventually my Driver's License. As part of our school coursework, the school system provided the class for free.

One valuable lesson that stuck deep in my memory was the importance of staying focused on my lane when driving at night. The instructor, Coach Mullin, said, "When you look at the oncoming headlights when a car is approaching (this is the part that stuck with me), you will drift where you look."

Isn't it amazing how the principles of life are true in every arena of life? Christine Caine writes, "God wants us to be diligent in keeping our eyes firmly fixed on Jesus—laser-focused.

He wants us to stay the course, because where we focus is where we'll go." [1]

It's no wonder the wise man wrote. "Let your eyes look straight ahead; fix your gaze directly before you." (Proverbs 4:25 NIV) It's easy to shift our focus when frightened, hurt, or lonely. That is when we always need to remember, "You drift where you look."

∽

Prayer

Jesus, I want to ask for Your help in keeping my focus on You in everything I do. When distractions come my way, remind me to look to You for guidance and strength. Let my heart and mind stay centered on You, so that I can live faithfully and reflect Your love every day. Amen.

∽

---

1. Caine, Christine. (2017) *Unshakeable*, p. 4. Grand Rapids: Zondervan.

32
WHEN I AM OVERWHELMED

"When I am overwhelmed, You alone know the way I should turn."
(Psalms 142:3)

"Then I pray to You, O Lord. I say, "You are my place of refuge. You are all I really want in life."
(Psalms 142:5)

The rescue of Mark Dickey from Turkey's Morca Cave mirrors the Psalmist's cry in Psalm 142. Dickey, who is an experienced American caver, was spelunking in 2023 in a deep cave when he became ill with stomach bleeding. Unable to ascend the 3281 feet to the surface, his situation was critical.

But hope was not lost for Mark. Over 190 experts from across Europe collaborated in a complex operation, navigating treacherous cave sections and setting up camps for his ascent.

Rescued after a week, Dickey thankfully said, "It is amazing to be above ground again."[1]

His words echo the Psalmist's when he, too, was hiding in a cave: "When I am overwhelmed, you alone know the way I should turn" (Psalms 142:3). The Hebrew word for "overwhelmed" describes the feeling of being engulfed by trials and tribulations, much like Dickey's experience in the cave.

We all, at some point, have those moments of being overwhelmed and feeling imprisoned by our current circumstances. But we also can testify as David, "Then I pray to you, O Lord. I say, 'You are my place of refuge. You are all I really want in life.'" These words, shared by many, can be a source of comfort and strength in our times of distress. (Psalms 142:5)

~

Prayer

Father, thank You for always helping me when I feel overwhelmed. Your comfort and strength mean everything to me. Please help me to always turn to You in those moments, trusting that You will provide the peace and guidance I need. Amen.

~

---

1. Ortiz, Jorge L. (2023) *"Mark Dickey: Turkey Cave Rescue."* USA Today. https://www.usatoday.com/story/news/investigations/2023/09/22/mark-dickey-turkey-cave-rescue/70911279007/.

33
WHY ORANGES ARE SOLD IN RED BAGS

"A new commandment I give unto you, That ye love one another; as I have loved you, that ye also love one another."
(John 13:34, KJV)

"By this shall all men know that ye are My disciples, if ye have love one to another."
(John 13:35, KJV)

Have you ever wondered why supermarkets sell oranges in red mesh bags? According to a 2019 article in Reader's Digest, the bags enhance the fruit's color, making it appear brighter and more appealing to consumers. This marketing strategy leverages the psychological effect of color contrast, as the red mesh complements the fruit's orange hue, making it stand out on the shelves.[1]

Jesus has given us our own "red mesh" bag to make us appear brighter and more appealing to the world. It is "love". "A new commandment I give unto you, That ye love one another; as I have loved you, that ye also love one another." (John 13:34)

Love sets us apart. Love amplifies our impact. Love complements our God-given gifts and abilities, making us "stand out" in the world. He added in the very next verse, "By this shall all men know that ye are my disciples, if ye have love one to another." (John 13:35)

∼

Prayer

Just as red bags make oranges more appealing, please help my love be such an example to the world that it attracts others to Jesus. Fill my heart with Your love so deeply that it overflows into every interaction I have. Let my actions and words reflect Your grace and kindness, attracting others to the beauty of knowing You. Amen.

∼

---

1. Landau, Sophie. (2023) *"This Is Why Oranges Are Sold in Red Mesh Bags."* Readers Digest. https://www.rd.com/article/oranges-red-mesh-bags/.

34
ELMO IS JUST CHECKING IN

"Cast all your cares on Him because He cares for you."
(1 Peter 5:7)

"Elmo is just checking in. How's everyone doing?" This tweet on Monday, January 29, 2024, from the "Elmo" account, elicited thousands of responses, with many expressing dismay and distress. Others shared feelings of joy and happiness. However, another sentiment also came out loud and clear in the replies: gratitude.

"Thanks for asking," wrote one person. "I am grateful for you, Elmo," chimed in another. Another person said, "Thanks for stopping by, bud."

In less than 48 hours, the post accumulated over 12,000 replies, garnered over 100,000 likes, and people reposted it over 46,000 times, as reported by Inc.com. On Tuesday, January 30, "Elmo" was the #1 trending topic in the U.S. on X (Twitter), with over 338,000 posts.

"Wow! Elmo is glad he asked!" responded the "Elmo" account on January 30. "Elmo learned it is important to ask a friend how they are doing."[1]

Elmo's tweet provides a powerful metaphor for God. He is always concerned about how we are doing. And unlike fleeting social media trends, God's presence is constant and unwavering, inviting us to come to Him with our burdens and find rest. "Cast all your cares on Him because He cares for you." (1 Peter 5:7)

God always asks, "How's everyone doing?" Even though He already knows, He loves to hear you tell Him. Why not go ahead and do that?

∼

Prayer

"Heavenly Father, I want to thank You for caring so deeply for me and being concerned about my needs. Your love and attention mean everything to me, and I'm grateful for Your constant presence in my life. Help me to always remember that You are watching over me and providing for every need I have. Amen.

∼

---

1. Shugerman, Emily. (2023) *"Elmo Tweets 'Checking In' on His Friends, Receives Flood of Distressed Responses."* People. people.com. https://people.com/elmo-tweets-checking-in-on-his-friends-receives-flood-of-distressed-responses-8553720.

35
SERVING INCONSPICUOUSLY

"So, my dear brothers and sisters, be strong and immovable. Always work enthusiastically for the Lord, for you know that nothing you do for the Lord is ever useless." (1 Corinthians 15:58)

The Gospels feature many quotes from well-known disciples like Peter and John. Thomas and Judas get their share of ink. Yet, James, the son of Alphaeus, remains conspicuously silent, with not a single quote attributed to him. He serves as a reminder that recognition in God's kingdom does not correlate with significance.

His life teaches us that staying faithful doesn't always come with recognition. He reminds us that our impact in the Kingdom isn't about how well-known we are but our constant dedication to Jesus.

Shirlene and I often attend different churches on Sundays because of our current ministry position. I am truly blessed by the genuine and humble people who love Jesus without commendations. These individuals keep the church doors open, fervently praying for the return of even one lost sheep. They deeply care for their communities, striving to be the guiding light that can transform their corner of the world. These saints raise their hands in worship of the God who has been their strength during tough weeks.

Each week, we meet people who live out the command of 1 Corinthians 15:58: "So, my dear brothers and sisters, be strong and immovable. Always work enthusiastically for the Lord, for you know that nothing you do for the Lord is ever useless." Can I repeat that last phrase? "You know that nothing you do for the Lord is ever useless."

Prayer

Jesus, I consider it the highest honor to serve You, even if my service goes unrecognized. Help me remember that my true reward is in pleasing You and not in seeking human praise. Give me the strength and humility to serve with joy and dedication, knowing that You see and value all that I do. Amen.

36
THE WORLD'S OLDEST TOY

"But God hath chosen the foolish things of the world to confound the wise; and God hath chosen the weak things of the world to confound the things which are mighty;"
(1 Corinthians 1:27)

Poohsticks is a game introduced by Winnie the Pooh, where two people drop a stick in a stream and see which one first reaches a predetermined finish line. A simple game involving...sticks! But did you know that in 2008, the National Toy Hall of Fame inducted the stick into its collection of the greatest toys?

According to their press release, the stick may be the world's oldest toy. Dogs play with them. In the hands of a child, a stick can become a sword, a fishing pole, a baton, a lightsaber, and a bat. Even adults will pick up a stick to draw in the sand. The

Hall of Fame concluded that sticks may not only "possibly be the oldest toys, they're possibly the best."[1]

As I read this article, I thought about how, if children can take the ordinary and, in their hands, make the extraordinary, how much more can the Almighty God take ordinary people like us and do extraordinary things? I am reminded of Paul's words, "But God hath chosen the foolish things of the world to confound the wise; and God hath chosen the weak things of the world to confound the things which are mighty." (1 Corinthians 1:27)

The next time you are walking and see a stick on the ground, remember the words of the National Toy Hall of Fame, "They're possibly the best." And, in His hand, so are you!

~

Prayer

Jesus, I thank You for seeing me as extraordinary, even when most people see me as ordinary. Your perspective and love mean everything to me. Help me live out my true worth in Your eyes, serving and loving others with the confidence that comes from knowing how deeply You value me. Amen.

~

---

1. Nuwer, Rachel. (2018) *"How a Stick Ended Up in the Toy Hall of Fame."* Outside. https://www.outsideonline.com/health/wellness/how-stick-ended-toy-hall-fame/.

❦ 37 ❦
KINDNESS CHANGES EVERYTHING

"If she says, 'Yes, have a drink, and I will water your camels, too!'—let her be the one...."
(Genesis 24:14)

"Don't forget to show hospitality to strangers, for some who have done this have entertained angels without realizing it!"
(Hebrews 13:2)

∽

Abraham tasked a servant to find a wife for his son, Isaac, sending the servant on an intriguing journey. The servant could have looked for someone beautiful, rich, or charming. Interestingly, he looked for someone who had the heart of a servant. "If she says, 'Yes, have a drink, and I will water your camels, too!'—let her be the one...." (Genesis 24:14)

Think about the story as if you didn't know the results. Rebekah didn't go to the well that day thinking she would become a part of the great lineage of the Hebrews, Abraham,

Isaac, and Jacob. Little did she know that her gift of hospitality would fulfill the purpose of God, not just for Isaac, but for the world. She was simply doing what she always did, and then a seemingly unimportant opportunity to be kind to a stranger presented itself. Being at the well was a demonstration of her faithful obedience. Being kind to the stranger was a demonstration of her generous demeanor. And the rest, as they say, is history!

You just never know what a small act of humility may accomplish, not only for yourself but for the surrounding multitudes. "Don't forget to show hospitality to strangers, for some who have done this have entertained angels without realizing it!" (Hebrews 13:2)

Prayer

Father, thank You for Your endless kindness. Help me show that same kindness to people around me, reflecting Your love in every interaction. Let my actions and words be filled with compassion and grace, making a positive impact on those I meet. Amen.

38
GOD'S RAG DOLL

"See how very much our Father loves us, for He calls us His children, and that is what we are!"
(1 John 3:1)

When our first child was born, Shirlene's maternal grandmother gave him a handmade set of stuffed "Three Bears": Papa, Mama, and Baby Bear. He loved the baby bear and would not sleep at night without him. Even as a two-year-old, Baby Bear was a nighttime companion. Of course, after enduring two years of being toted around by a learning-to-walk infant, nighttime drools, and every other imaginable infant-induced abuse, Baby Bear became stained, with seams coming apart, and faded.

But we never considered throwing Baby Bear out, even though he had any inherent value. Time had caused him to become torn, stained, and faded. Baby Bear's value was not intrinsic. He was valuable because of who loved him. To everyone else, it was a stained, torn, and ragged stuffed animal.

But our son's love for Baby Bear gave it immeasurable value. If you loved Michael, you loved Baby Bear.

The analogy is obvious. You may feel ragged, torn, and stained. In others' eyes, you may appear worthless. But in your moment of struggle, hear the words of the beloved disciple, John, "See how very much our Father loves us, for he calls us his children, and that is what we are!" (1 John 3:1) Your value is not in your perfection, your purity, or your abilities. Your value comes from the love of Someone who cares about you.

∾

Prayer

Father, I appreciate your deep love for me, even though I have experienced brokenness and the stains of sin. Your love and grace give my life meaning and purpose. Help me to always remember that Your love is a gift, and let it inspire me to live in a way that honors You. Amen.

∾

39

GET UP AND PRAISE THE LORD

"The wicked flee when no one pursues, but the righteous are bold as a lion."
(Psalm 28:1)

According to a BBC report, a lion's roar carries over five miles. Its powerful and majestic roar is not just by chance. The report says that the lion has unique vocal cords, which allow its roar to be heard far away. A lion's roar serves as a means of marking its territory, communicating with other lions, and scaring potential threats.[1]

Proverbs 28:1 states, "The wicked flee when no one pursues, but the righteous are bold as a lion." Like a lion roaring in a

---

1. BBC. (n.d.) "Nine Roar-some Facts About Lions," BBC.com. https://www.bbc.co.uk/programmes/articles/1WXqfwCNlzqwLTQfMTDSgY5/nine-roar-some-facts-about-lions#:-:text=A%20lion's%20roar%20can%20be%20heard%20-five%20miles%20away&text=It's%20so%20loud%20it%20-can,shape%20of%20the%20cat's%20larynx.

savannah, we have the opportunity, through praise, to let the world hear of our great God. The wise man describes the confidence and boldness that comes from living a righteous life. The lion's roar expresses its inherent power. Our worship expresses the power and majesty of our God.

Our voices, lifted in unison, can create a symphony of adoration that reaches far and wide, touching hearts and transforming lives.

> "So come on, my soul,
> Oh, don't you get shy on me
> Lift up your song,
> 'Cause you've got a LION
> Inside of those lungs
> Get up and praise the Lord."[2]

∼

Prayer

"Jesus, I worship and praise You with all my heart. Your goodness and love fill me with awe, and I want to honor You in everything I do. May I live a life of constant worship, reflecting Your glory and spreading Your light wherever I go. Amen.

∼

---

2. Lake, Brandon. (2020) "Gratitude." Bethel Music.

40
KIND WORDS

"Kind words are like honey—sweet to the soul and healthy for the body."
(Proverbs 16:24)

"And I tell you this, you must give an account on judgment day for every idle word you speak. The words you say will either acquit you or condemn you."
(Matthew 12:36-37)

Have you ever wondered if honey has an expiration date? Well, despite what you might find on the bottle's label, honey has the incredible ability to last forever.

Archaeologists once sampled honey from 3,000-year-old Egyptian tombs and found it was still good to eat! The ancient Egyptians used honey not just as a sweetener, but also as a preservative.[1]

---

1. Darren Incorvaia. (August 15, 2021) *"Honey's Eternal Shelf Life, Explained."*

Proverbs 16:24 beautifully states, "Kind words are like honey—sweet to the soul and healthy for the body." Just as honey remains a timeless delight, kind and pleasant words never lose their power to nourish others. We should never underestimate the power of words. As a child, we often taunted others by saying, "Sticks and stones may break my bones, but words will never hurt me." But they do. They can wound and create division. Conversely, words can open doors and break down barriers.

Jesus tells us in Matthew 12:36, 37, "And I tell you this, you must give an account on judgment day for every idle word you speak. The words you say will either acquit you or condemn you." As believers, we should use our words to preserve and sweeten the world.

∽

Prayer

Holy Spirit, guard my words so they can encourage and sweeten the world around me. Let everything I say be filled with kindness, love, and truth, reflecting You. Help me use my speech to lift others up and bring Your light into every conversation. Amen.

∽

DiscoverMagazine.com. Darren Incorvaia. "Honey's Eternal Shelf Life, Explained." Discover Magazine. https://www.discovermagazine.com/planet-earth/honeys-eternal-shelf-life-explained

41
SOARING LIKE EAGLES

"They that wait upon the LORD shall renew their strength; they shall mount up with wings as eagles."
(Isaiah 40:31)

When an eagle gets too close to the nests of smaller birds, the smaller birds will "mob" attack the eagle in the air. Because they are smaller and more agile, the eagle is at a significant disadvantage. However, rather than fight the smaller birds, the eagle soars to a higher atmosphere. Higher than the smaller birds can survive.

Don't miss the valuable lesson God provides us in the eagle. The eagle doesn't waste energy fighting the smaller birds, nor does it spend time screeching to the smaller birds of its own majesty. It never has to tell the other birds that it is an eagle. Eagles simply ascend to greater heights, leaving their troubles below.

It is easy to engage in verbal sparring matches to defend

ourselves. We can belittle others because we feel their attacks have diminished our worth. But that seldom produces anything significant in our personal and interpersonal relationships.

It gives new meaning to the great encouragement in Isaiah 40:31: "They that wait upon the LORD shall renew their strength; they shall mount up with wings as eagles." May we refuse to waste our energies on trivial matters or our breath trying to convince people of our majesty. Let's mount up with wings and allow the Lord to renew our strength.

∼

Prayer

Lord, help me soar above the fray of others' attacks, just like an eagle soars above the attacks of smaller birds. Give me the strength and wisdom to rise above negativity and criticism, keeping my focus on You. Help me maintain grace and dignity, trusting in Your protection and guidance. Amen.

∼

42

EYES ON THE BANNER

But You have raised a banner for those who fear you— a rallying point in the face of attack."
(Psalms 60:4)

"His banner over me was love."
(Song of Solomon 2:4 KJV)

Life is certainly not always a playground. Often it reflects a battleground. Relational battles. Emotional battles. Spiritual battles. Financial battles. Have you ever felt like you're not winning the battle?

David wrote Psalm 60 when his kingdom was experiencing a tough battle. The superscription before verse 1 indicates that David's troops were fighting the Aramaeans in the north. The Edomites were attacking from the south according to 2 Samuel 8. As the opposing forces pinch the armies of Israel, with defeat appearing imminent, David bursts forth in song, "But you have raised a banner for those who fear you — a rallying point in the face of attack." (Psalms 60:4)

The Christ-Centered Exposition Commentary says this about a banner: "A signal flag was a type of standard or banner often used in war to be a rallying point for the troops. It was visible during battle and, therefore, served as an encouragement and motivation for the soldiers." [1]

During the battle, the troops would look to the banner, renewing their spirits and their commitment. David's son, Solomon, must have heard the stories of the rally banners, for he would write later, "His banner over me was love." (Song of Solomon 2:4 KJV)

May I remind you today, regardless of your battle, to cast your eyes on the banner of His love and find encouragement and renewal.

∼

Prayer

Father, thank You for raising a banner for those who fear You, as You've promised in Psalm 60:4. Help me look to Your banner of truth and find courage and strength, especially during tough times. Let my heart be filled with trust and praise, knowing You are my protector and guide. Amen.

∼

---

1. Akin, Daniel L., David Platt, and Tony Merida. (2017) *Psalm 60:4 - Run To Your Deliverer.* Christ-Centered Exposition Commentary: Exalting Jesus in Psalms 51-100. Nashville: B&H Publishing Group.

43

A TIME FOR DELIGHT

"There is a season (a time appointed) for everything and a time for every delight and event or purpose under heaven."
(Ecclesiastes 3:1, The Amplified Bible)

∽

On March 18, 2024, the New York Post told the story of Madeline, a 9-year-old from Benton, Arkansas, who had a cool moment. She found a pink grasshopper while walking to her family barn. "When I was littler I saw one in a book," Madeline told a local news station. "I thought it would be cool to have."[1]

For the average person, a grasshopper wouldn't catch our attention, but for Madeline, it was like finding a diamond. Entomologists say that only 1% of grasshoppers are pink.

I wonder how often we overlook the small things that, if we

---

1. Propper, David. (March 18, 2024). *"9-Year-Old Bug Expert Discovers and Captures Super Rare Pink Grasshopper."* New York Post. https://nypost.com/2024/03/18/us-news/9-year-old-bug-expert-discovers-and-captures-super-rare-pink-grasshopper/.

took the time to notice, would be really "cool"? I love the way the Amplified Bible states Ecclesiastes 3:1: "There is a season (a time appointed) for everything and a time for every delight and event or purpose under heaven."

We often focus on the first part of that verse, but I love there is "a time for every delight". I want to discipline myself today to take time for a delight under heaven. I believe God provides us with many opportunities to experience delight. Unfortunately, we miss them because of current stress, obnoxious people, or the pressures of life. But may we never forget that God has designed a time for every delight.

∽

Prayer
Father, thank You for designing a time for every delight, as described in Ecclesiastes. Your perfect timing brings beauty and purpose to my life. Help me trust in Your plan and enjoy each season You've created for me. Amen.

∽

44
AT JUST THE RIGHT TIME

"And we know that God causes everything to work together for the good of those who love God and are called according to his purpose for them."
(Romans 8:28)

In the movie "Apollo 13", NASA works tirelessly to bring the Apollo spacecraft and its three astronauts back to Earth safely after an oxygen tank explodes in the service module just two days into the mission, creating an almost impossible challenge.

During the movie, a team member outlines all the issues that could go wrong to one official, who then remarks, "This may be the worst crisis NASA has ever faced." At that moment, flight director Gene Kranz interjects, "Respectfully, sir, I believe this will be our finest moment."

That last statement epitomizes the trust we, as believers, have in God. We recognize we are not exempt from struggles, heartaches, betrayals, sickness, or loss. But rather than believing life's difficulties "could be the worst disaster" we have experienced, we trust that this is "going to be our finest hour."

"And we know that God causes everything to work together for the good of those who love God and are called according to his purpose for them." (Romans 8:28)

Because of that knowledge, we can sing:

> I trust in God, my Savior
> The One who will never fail.
> I sought the Lord
> And He heard, and He answered
> That's why I trust Him.
> And He heard and He answered
> That's why I trust Him. [1]

∼

Prayer

Heavenly Father, strengthen me to not give up when I'm weary. Help me trust that at just the right time, You will provide an answer. Your faithfulness gives me hope, and I believe You to work all things together for my good. Amen.

∼

---

1. Lake, Brandon; Brown, Christopher Joel; Wong, Mitch; and Furtick, Steven. (2023) *"I Trust in God."* Elevation Worship.

45
IT'S THE LITTLE THINGS

"And if you give even a cup of cold water to one of the least of my followers, you will surely be rewarded."
(Matthew 10:42)

On February 13, 2024, a father posted on X (formerly Twitter),

"My toddler left his toy at an @IHGhotels while traveling. We called them, and they said they would get it in the mail for us."

But the hotel went far beyond that. The hotel desk clerk took several pictures of the Beanie Baby, named "Snuggle Puppy", at different places throughout the hotel and mailed them to the father, explaining to the toddler that Snuggle Puppy was well and would soon be home. Also, they jokingly said they had put the toy to work until he caught his ride home.

The toddler laughed as he saw his beloved stuffed toy

"working" at different places throughout the hotel and was relieved to learn that Snuggle Puppy would soon be home.[1]

Creating the pictures was a small act of kindness that didn't seem that significant. But a young boy will grow up with a lifelong memory of a desk clerk who cared enough to comfort his loss.

"And if you give even a cup of cold water to one of the least of my followers, you will surely be rewarded." (Matthew 10:42) In a culture that applauds the grandiose and spectacular, may I remember God applauds the simple and seemingly insignificant. Can you imagine the impact in our world if every Believer did one small, insignificant act to make someone's day better today? Even a cup of cold water or sending pictures of some child's favorite Beanie Baby.

∼

Prayer

Holy Spirit, I ask for the wisdom to see and do small tasks that can help others. Help me to recognize the little ways I can make a difference and serve those around me. Give me a heart full of compassion and a willingness to act, knowing that even small acts of kindness can have a big impact. Amen.

∼

---

1. Murphy, Bill Jr. (February 15, 2024) *"A Toddler Lost a Special Toy at Holiday Inn Express. The Response Was a Stroke of Genius."* Inc. https://www.inc.com/bill-murphy-jr/a-toddler-lost-a-special-toy-at-holiday-inn-express-response-was-a-stroke-of-genius.html#:~:text=In%20short%2C%20the%20workers%20at,laugh%20out%20of%20the%20experience.

46

THE ONE WHO ENDURES

"Let us run with perseverance the race marked out for us."
(Hebrews 12:1 NIV)

"But the one who endures to the end will be saved."
(Matthew 24:13)

In the 2023 South East Asia 500-meter race, a Cambodian runner named Bou Samnang provided an amazing example of endurance under difficult circumstances. It wasn't because she won the race. In fact, she finished last. What was remarkable was the fact that in a monsoonal downpour, her spirit remained unbroken. The crowd that was watching cheered on her resilient spirit, despite finishing the race six minutes behind the other racers. Bou also struggles with anemia, which slowed her down tremendously. [1]

---

1. Chappell, Bill. (May 16, 2023) *"Cambodian Female Runner Finishes Last but*

Bou Samnang's philosophy, "I tried to reach the finish line because I wanted to show people that in life, even though we go a bit slow or fast, we will reach our destination all the same."

The writer of Hebrews uses the word "perseverance" when describing our race to spend eternity with Jesus. "Let us run with perseverance the race marked out for us." (Hebrews 12:1 NIV)

As you continue in your race today, despite the rain you may experience, always remember "the fastest runner doesn't always win the race, and the strongest warrior doesn't always win the battle." (Ecclesiastes 9:11) "But the one who endures to the end will be saved." (Matthew 24:13) Just take another step today.

Prayer

Father, thank You for giving me the strength to endure to the end of the race. Help me keep my eyes on You and to persevere through every challenge. Fill me with Your endurance and faith, so I can finish strong and bring glory to Your name. Amen.

Celebrates in the Rain at Southeast Asian Games" NPR. https://www.npr.org/2023/05/16/1176430543/female-runner-cambodia-last-rain-southeast-asian-games

47
GRANDMA SHIPHRAH AND GRANDMA PUAH

"I tell you the truth, if you had faith even as small as a mustard seed, you could say to this mountain, 'Move from here to there,' and it would move. Nothing would be impossible."
(Matthew 17:20)

∽

I can imagine two families huddled together on the day Israel left Egypt after 430 years (Exodus 12:40-41). The great-grandmothers of both families were probably dead. Still, I am sure that as the families gathered around one another beginning the journey to the Promised Land, they remembered Grandma Shiphrah and Grandma Puah (Exodus 1:15-21). And each family said a word of grateful praise for the matriarchs of their families.

Little did these two ladies know that when they risked their own lives to save the Hebrew baby boys some 80 years before, one baby would be Moses, the promised deliverer. I am sure that as Moses' family members looked to the front of the crowd of Hebrews and saw the man with the staff leading them to freedom, they couldn't help but reflect with a bit of family pride about their grandmothers. There may not have been a Moses if it had not been for the Grandma Shiphrah and Grandma Puah!

The thing about our choices today is...you just never know. Our commitment to obeying Him will have a profound effect on our immediate family and future generations. Right now, it may appear insignificant. However, God has an amazing way of taking small acts of obedience and creating magnificent results. "I tell you the truth, if you had faith even as small as a mustard seed, you could say to this mountain, 'Move from here to there,' and it would move. Nothing would be impossible." May there come a day when future generations will look back with thanksgiving for our lives today.

Prayer

I know You specialize in taking small steps of obedience and turning them into magnificent results in the future. Like you did with Shiphrah and Puah, may Your power and grace transform even my tiniest efforts into something extraordinary. Help me trust in Your plan and continue to follow Your lead, knowing that You are working through me in amazing ways. Amen.

48
THE GOD WHO SEES

"You are El-Roi (The God Who Sees Me)."
(Genesis 16:13)

She seemed to be a person of no value. Probably given to Sarai by Pharaoh as a penitence for unknowingly claiming Abram's wife for his harem, she was accustomed to being traded as a commodity. Given away by Sarai to her husband Abraham to fulfill a seemingly unanswered promise, she is again a pawn in the plans of others. After being impregnated by Abram, her former owner becomes jealous and devious. The father of her child fails to stand in her defense. She has had enough.

Hagar runs away. Hurt and abused, it seemed no one valued her for who she was...a person created in the image of God. Others simply saw her as a tool to receive what they wanted—a person with little value except for what she could do for them.

But at a cool, refreshing water spot in a desert, God showed up for this simple, pregnant woman with a message just for her.

He noticed her struggles when nobody else did. He saw her for who she was – a human, a mom-to-be, a woman worthy of having her own family tree.

And Hagar worshiped, "You are El-Roi (The God Who Sees Me)." (Genesis 16:13)

May you always remember, in times of isolation, in moments of distress, when your heart is broken, that He is still El-Roi!

Prayer

Thank You for seeing me not as others do but as a person of great value, just like You did with Hagar. Your perspective fills me with worth and dignity. Help me embrace Your view of me and live confidently, knowing You see my true value and love me deeply. Help me see others in the same manner. Amen.

49
YOU ARE...MINE

"Do not be afraid, for I have ransomed you. I have called you by name; you are mine."
(Isaiah 43:1)

~

Have you ever noticed how many great movie lines are declarations of identity? "I am Spartacus!" "I am your father." "I'm the king of the world!"

There is a motivation within each of us to declare our identity. Because of my name, I can identify as a member of a tribe, the Stones. Because of my age, I can identify with the AARP crowd. Because of my height, I can identify with the "don't fit in airline seats" group.

But I love how Christine Caine, in her book "Undaunted" parses Isaiah 43:1. While her punctuation may not be accurate, the concept is wonderful. She provides us with the greatest descriptor any of us could desire. Today, I pray you will claim it, embrace it, and find encouragement in it.

"I have called you by name; you are… 'Mine'." (It actually says, "I have called you by name; you are mine.")[1]

What better name could God give you than "Mine"? Since He has called us by that name, we should always find hope in that we belong to His family, that we are under His care, and that His provision covers us.

∾

Prayer
Heavenly Father, I thank You for calling me Your child and for Your incredible care and provision. Your love and support mean everything to me. Help me to always remember my identity in You and trust in Your faithful provision for all my needs. Amen.

∾

---

1. Caine, Christine. (2012) Undaunted, p. 62. Grand Rapids: Zondervan

50

A PRISONER OF HOPE

"Return to your fortress, you prisoners of hope."
(Zechariah 9:12 NIV)

After 70 years of imprisonment in Babylon, the people of Judah were finally coming home to Jerusalem. They had been prisoners in a foreign land for most of their lives, and they understood the term "prisoners."

Through the prophet Zechariah, God calls them an intriguing name. "Return to your fortress, you prisoners of hope." (Zechariah 9:12) Prisoners? Hope? Talk about an oxymoron! Those two terms don't normally go together.

The Hebrew term for "prisoners" means "those who are bound or restricted"[1]. The word "hope" signifies "a cord or

---

1. Bible Hub. (n.d.) "Hebrew: 615. asir." [https://biblehub.com/hebrew/615.htm] (https://biblehub.com/hebrew/615.htm).

expectation"[2]. It implies being tethered to something unshakeable. God's descriptor of "prisoners of hope" describes a people who, during difficulties, are bound and restricted by... hope.

Far too many Christians are prisoners of despair, past hurts, and pessimism. In His call to "return to your fortress", God reminds us that our hope is not in the condition of society. Nor how others treat us. Or even the performance of other Christians. Our cord of hope finds its anchor in the fortress of our Mighty God. He never changes. He never fails. May I be a prisoner of hope and, as the old hymn says,

> I've anchored in Jesus
> The storms of life I'll brave
> I've anchored in Jesus
> I'll fear no wind or wave
> I've anchored in Jesus
> For He has power to save
> I've anchored in the Rock of Ages[3]

Prayer

Jesus, You are my hope even when things are difficult. I anchor my hope in You, and Your love and strength keep me steady through every storm. Help me hold to this hope and trust in Your faithfulness, no matter what challenges I face. Amen.

2.

3. Jones, Lewis. (1901) I've Anchored in Jesus. Public Domain.

51

REDEMPTION IN FAILURE

"The sailors were awestruck by the Lord's great power, and they offered him a sacrifice and vowed to serve him."
(Jonah 1:16)

None of us are immune to failure. Unfortunately, our spiritual enemy is a master at condemning our usefulness because of our failure. He loves to remind us that our failures disqualify us from being used by God. But the story of Jonah reveals an often-forgotten truth: God can turn even our failures into opportunities for His glory.

After the great storm threatened to destroy the ship Jonah had taken to avoid going to Ninevah, the sailors threw Jonah into the sea, and the sea miraculously calmed down. Then something extraordinary happened! "The sailors were awestruck by the Lord's great power, and they offered him a sacrifice and vowed to serve him." (Jonah 1:16). The Hebrew word for "awestruck" reveals a faith born from witnessing God's power. [1]

Jonah's flight from God unexpectedly led these sailors to a life-changing encounter. It is an excellent reminder of how God's plans prevail, even through our failures. In our lives, mistakes and missteps can become Divine intersections where God can and will show Himself mighty. He is a Master Designer who can take our imperfections and weave them into the greater tapestry of His redemptive work.

Prayer

Father, thank you for using me even when I fail. My mistakes and shortcomings do not disqualify me from Your plans. Help me trust in Your grace and know that You can still work through me, turning my failures into opportunities for growth and service. Amen.

---

1. BibleHub. "Jonah 1:6 Hebrew Text Analysis." BibleHub, accessed June 19, 2024. https://biblehub.com/text/jonah/1-6.htm.
   Bible Study Tools. "Jonah 1:6 Interlinear Bible." Bible Study Tools, accessed June 19, 2024. https://www.biblestudytools.com/interlinear-bible/passage/?q=Jonah+1%3A6.

52
THIS IS A TEST

"Blessed is the one who perseveres under trial because, having stood the test, that person will receive the crown of life that the Lord has promised to those who love Him."
(James 1:12 NIV)

Do you remember taking tests when you were in school? Typically, other than offering some essential instructions, your teacher remained silent. This wasn't a time for instruction. It was a time to evaluate and observe your knowledge. An excellent instructor would use those evaluations to reinforce areas of competency and improve areas of deficiency.

Sometimes, during times of our trials and tests, God seems silent. But those moments are never a sign of absence, but of a Divine teaching moment. James tells us, "Blessed is the one who perseveres under trial because, having stood the test, that person will receive the crown of life that the Lord has promised to those who love Him." (James 1:12)

He reminds us that our tests are not obstacles but growth opportunities. The word "test" is *peirasmos* and suggests a process intended to refine or strengthen.[1] In these moments of testing, our faith is refined and our character shaped. The test should strengthen us, not destroy us. That is why James says we are "blessed" when we stay under the fire of the trial.

Prayer

Jesus, I recognize that the tests of life refine and strengthen me. Help me remember these challenges are shaping me into who You want me to be. Give me the courage and patience to face each test with faith, knowing that You are strengthening me and making me more resilient. Amen.

---

1. Bible Hub. (n.d.) "Greek: 3986. peirasmos." [https://biblehub.com/greek/3986.html](https://biblehub.com/greek/3986.htm).

53
A DOOR OF HOPE

"I will give her [Israel]...the Valley of Achor as a door of hope."
(Hosea 2:15 NKJV)

"...give them beauty for ashes, The oil of joy for mourning, The garment of praise for the spirit of heaviness."
(Isaiah 61:3 NKJV)

~

In the middle of a lesson concerning His steadfast love for us through the example of Hosea and his prostitute wife, Gomer, God also provided us with one of the most beautiful promises in Scripture, "I will give her [Israel]...the Valley of Achor as a door of hope." (Hosea 2:15)

Centuries before, they executed Achan and his followers in the Valley of Achor because of their rebellion. (Joshua 7:24-26)

The word "Achor" means "trouble".[1] This place brought painful memories for Israel. But God says He will transform the "Valley of Trouble" into a "Door of Hope".

What a wonderful promise for us today. In His hands, places of desolation and difficult memories, like Achor, can become places of hope. He is still a God who can "give them beauty for ashes, the oil of joy for mourning, the garment of praise for the spirit of heaviness." (Isaiah 61:3) That is the essence of His steadfast love. When we are experiencing ashes, mourning, and heaviness, because of His love, He gives us beauty, joy, and a spirit of praise.

If you are in a valley of trouble today, keep looking. The door is opening!

∼

Prayer

Thank You for showing me a door of hope in my valleys of trouble. Your guidance and love turn my hardest times into opportunities for growth, renewal, and blessings. Help me trust in Your ability to bring hope and light into every difficult situation. Amen.

∼

---

1. Bible Hub. (n.d.) "Strong's Hebrew: 5911. עָכוֹר (Achor)." https://biblehub.com/hebrew/5911.htm.

54

TURNING YOUR FACE AGAINST THE WIND

"But continue thou in the things which thou hast learned and hast been assured of..."
(1 Timothy 3:14, KJV)

"If ye ABIDE in Me and My words ABIDE in you..."
(John 15:7, KJV)

In 2 Timothy 3:14, Paul uses a powerful Greek word, *mene*, which translates as "continue." [1] "But continue thou in the things which thou hast learned and hast been assured of..." Jesus used the same word in John 15 when he said, "If you ABIDE in Me and My words ABIDE in you...." [2]

Paul calls Timothy and all of us to stay true to our faith

---

1. Bible Hub. (n.d.) "Strong's Greek: 3306. μένω (menó)." https://biblehub.com/greek/3306.htm.
2. BibleHub. (n.d.) "Strong's Greek: 3306. μένω (menó)." Retrieved from https://biblehub.com/greek/3306.htm.

despite what is happening around us. Paul writes these words to this young pastor in Ephesus whose church is experiencing persecution and decline. Additionally, Paul, confined in prison, writes these words to Timothy, reminding him to remain steadfast. Both are experiencing extreme difficulties.

This word mene isn't just about continuing; it's a more profound encouragement to persist and hold firm, no matter what. Regardless of the storms blowing around us, it is an invitation to anchor ourselves and stand firm and unwavering in our faith. It is a fruit of the Spirit, perseverance or long-suffering. There will be times when all we can do is simply put our heads down against the wind and push forward. It is the testimony of those who endure difficulties and receive the reward at the end of the race.

∽

Prayer

Heaven Father, I desire to be an example of abiding, enduring, and persevering through the difficulties of life. Your presence sustains me through every challenge and trial. Help me remain steadfast in my faith, trusting that You will carry me through and bring me victory in Your time. Amen.

∽

55
MY WALMART EXPERIENCE

"For God is not unjust. He will not forget how hard you have worked for Him and how you have shown your love to him by caring for other believers, as you still do."
(Hebrews 6:10)

A while back, I had an unusual experience at Walmart. I was trying to purchase a book light for my wife, and I was having difficulty finding the book section (remember when it used to be prominently towards the front of the store).

My phone's Walmart app told me it was at a specific aisle, but when I went there...it wasn't there. Walking back and forth to see if I was missing it, a Walmart associate, probably 75 years old and stocking some items in a nearby aisle, asked me, "Can I help you find something?" I told her I was looking for the book section, and she said, "You're about 15 miles in the wrong direction. Come with me, and I'll show you."

She started walking, with a limp, in the opposite direction. I assured her I could find it if she just pointed me in the right direction, but she just kept walking. So, I followed and arrived to find the section I wanted. As I thanked her for her tremendous customer service, she began walking back to the opposite side of the store and said, "That's what I'm here to do. Help our customers."

When I returned to my truck, I had so many convicting thoughts. What if every time I walked into a church, I looked for opportunities to serve my fellow worshipers? What if, when driving in congested traffic, I saw opportunities to help other drivers? What if, when walking in the door of my home, I looked to serve my family?

God notices when we serve others! "For God is not unjust. He will not forget how hard you have worked for Him and how you have shown your love to him by caring for other believers, as you still do." (Hebrews 6:10). Don't miss it, and don't forget it! We show our love to Him by caring for others.

Prayer

Jesus, I know I show my love for You by loving others. Help me reflect and demonstrate Your compassion and kindness in all my interactions. Fill my heart with Your love so that I can be an authentic example of Your love to everyone I meet. Amen.

56

FOR ALL THE "DUKES" IN THE WORLD

"He calls His own sheep by name."
(John 10:3)

Each year, the U.S. government's Social Security website releases the ten most popular baby names in the United States. Number one in 2022? Liam for baby boys and Olivia for baby girls. Duke was nowhere to be found on the list. In fact, the number of baby boys named Duke in the U.S. in 2022 was only 399. I didn't think it was necessary to check how many girls were named after me. I offered the name "Dukelene" (a combination of my and my wife's names) to all our granddaughters when they were born, but no one accepted.

Growing up with this name, you can imagine the inferences made as peers made rhymes with it (I'll save you the gross terms). Two of my brothers will tell you that I was named after a gorilla in the Tulsa, OK, zoo (but if they are pressed, they will finally admit that one of them was a huge Dodgers fan, and for some reason, my parents allowed him to name me after one of the Dodger legends, Duke Snyder).

As an adult, when I tell strangers my name, I am often greeted with, "That sounds like a movie star's name.", or "What a strong name." Amazingly, my feelings toward my name changed as the descriptors of others changed.

Doing some rough math, the numbers show that even though "Duke" will never be one of the most popular names for baby boys, in the course of a 70-year period, there are around 21,000 of us running around the U.S. Every once in a while, I meet one of those special guys.

And even though "Duke" will probably never be the most popular name in the United States, I find comfort in knowing that Jesus "calls His own sheep by name." (John 10:3) Not only does He know each of us by name, He knows each of us who shares a name intimately. Yes, He even knows you used to have a dog named "Duke".

Prayer

Jesus, what a privilege it is to know you know me by name. Your intimate knowledge of me fills me with gratitude and awe. Help me to always remember that I am personally known and loved by You, and let that truth guide my every step. Amen.

57
GOD AND OREO COOKIES

"Jesus Christ is the same yesterday and today and forever."
(Hebrews 13:8)

The New York Times had a story about an MIT study that twisted open over 1,000 Oreo cookies to see if you could twist them in such a way that the cream in the middle would attach itself to both wafers. They had a machine twist them in ways that took fractions of a second to over five minutes.[1]

My first thought, like yours, is probably, "Who cares? Isn't there something more important they ought to be researching?" (By the way, over 80% of the time, no matter how you twist an Oreo cookie, the cream stays on one wafer. Just in case you were laying awake at night stressing over it.)

---

1. Holt, Kris. (April 19, 2022) *MIT Researchers Build Device to Study Oreo Cookie Cream.* Engadget. https://www.engadget.com/mit-oreo-cookie-cream-device-because-science-175016653.html.

However, the cookie twist study reminds me of a truth in which I find hope, strength, and gratitude. Hebrews 13:8 says, "Jesus Christ is the same yesterday and today and forever." There is not a lot in life that is consistent. The weather changes. The economy changes. Feelings change. But Jesus Christ is the same! Regardless of how life turns, I am thankful I can trust that God's love, grace, and mercy remain unwavering. When the world around me feels chaotic and unpredictable, I find peace in knowing that God is completely consistent, even more so than the twist of an Oreo cookie.

Prayer

Jesus, what a comfort it is to know that You are the same yesterday, today, and forever. Your unchanging nature gives me stability and hope in an ever-changing world. Help me to always rely on Your constant love and faithfulness. Amen.

58
PEOPLE USED TO SAY

"What's more, your relative Elizabeth has become pregnant in her old age! People used to say she was barren, but she has conceived a son and is now in her sixth month. For the word of God will never fail."
(Luke 1:36-37)

"Awe fell upon the whole neighborhood, and the news of what had happened spread throughout the Judean hills. Everyone who heard about it reflected on these events and asked, "What will this child turn out to be?" For the hand of the Lord was surely upon him in a special way."
(Luke 1:65-66)

There is a little line tucked away in the early incarnation story of Jesus that we sometimes miss. It is actually contained in the birth story of John to Elizabeth and Zacharias. When the angel Gabriel came to tell Mary that she had been chosen to give birth to the Savior of the world, he also informed her that her elderly, barren cousin Elizabeth would give birth to a son as well. We know that son as John the Baptist. As Gabriel tells Mary about her immaculate conception, he says this about Elizabeth in Luke 1:36-37, "What's more, your relative Elizabeth has become pregnant in her old age! People used to say she was barren, but she has conceived a son and is now in her sixth month. For the word of God will never fail." The King James version says, "For nothing is impossible with God."

Don't miss this little phrase in verse 36: "People used to say she was barren." There was so much shame attached to barrenness in Elizabeth's day. Apparently, the people around her didn't mind saying that she was barren.

Do you believe God can change the story of your life? Are you hopeful and expectant? People may say negative things or think negative thoughts, but their limited perspectives should not impact your faith. Nothing is impossible with God.

As He often does, God called Elizabeth to wait longer than most to see her dream fulfilled, because the answer to her prayers served a greater purpose than she could imagine. Others' words may hurt, discourage, or even anger us, but may we never forget the storyline of Elizabeth. "People used to say…"

Then, verses 65-66 of Luke 1 tell us about those same people: "Awe fell upon the whole neighborhood, and the news of what had happened spread throughout the Judean hills. Everyone who heard about it reflected on these events and asked, 'What will this child turn out to be?' For the hand of the Lord was surely upon him in a special way."

When people say something hurtful about you, be careful with your response. Try not to let their words discourage you. Remember, when someone speaks negatively about you, the word of God will never fail. Nothing is impossible with God. And the same ones who talk about you now will one day be in awe of God's favor in your life.

Prayer

God, You have the incredible ability to change what shames me to that which brings You glory. Your transformative power renews my heart and life. Help me embrace Your work in me so I can reflect Your glory in all I do. Amen.

59
HEARING FROM HOME

"Do not let your hearts be troubled. You believe in God, believe also in me. My Father's house has many rooms; if that were not so, would I have told you that I am going there to prepare a place for you? And if I go and prepare a place for you, I will come back and take you to be with Me that you also may be where I am."
(John 14:1-3, NIV)

Henri Nouwen recounts the story of a soldier who became a prisoner of war. His captors transported him by train far from his homeland. He felt isolated from the country, parted from his family, void of anything familiar. His loneliness grew as he continued not to hear anything from home. He could not know whether his family was even alive, or how his country was faring. He had lost a sense of anything to live for.

But suddenly, unexpectedly, he got a letter. Months of travel had left the letter with smudges and torn edges. But it said, "We are waiting for you to come home. All is fine here. Don't worry."

Everything instantly seemed different. His circumstances had not changed. He did the same difficult labor on the same meager rations, but now he knew someone waited for his release and homecoming. Hope changed his life. [1]

Jesus left us with a letter of hope as well. He knew we would experience moments when we felt alone, isolated, captured by the circumstances we were experiencing. He knew those times would be thieves attempting to rob us of all hope. So before He went back to the Father, He sent us a word of hope found in John 14:1-3, "Do not let your hearts be troubled. You believe in God, believe also in Me. My Father's house has many rooms; if that were not so, would I have told you that I am going there to prepare a place for you? And if I go and prepare a place for you, I will come back and take you to be with me that you also may be where I am."

And so today, regardless of the circumstances you find yourself in, hear the words of your Savior encouraging you from heaven, "We are waiting for you to come home. All is fine here. Don't worry."

Prayer

Holy Spirit, there are times I need to hear from You when I'm struggling. Your words bring comfort, guidance, and strength in my toughest times. Help me listen closely and rely on Your voice to lead me through every challenge. Amen.

---

[1]. Nouwen, Henri. (2006). Spiritual Direction: Wisdom for the Long Walk Home, p.. 100. New York: HarperOne

60

WHEN YOU HAVE DOUBTS

"He sent his disciples to ask Jesus, "Are you the Messiah we've been expecting, or should we keep looking for someone else?"
(Matthew 11:2-3)

"I tell you the truth, of all who have ever lived, none is greater than John the Baptist."
(Matthew 11:11)

If we could travel back to ancient Judea to a Roman prison cell, we could look through the door's small window and see a man on the floor. He has just started history's biggest revolution. His words have started a movement that will last for over two thousand years. Future historians will describe him as courageous, noble, and visionary.

We would think that John the Baptist never doubted anything. He was always sure of what he believed and never hesitated to share his beliefs with others. He was like the sun in the desert - strong and unwavering.

Until now. This is the part of the story where John faces death. He doesn't feel as brave as he did before, and he's not sure what to do. The clouds come, and it becomes dark. In his final moments, he doesn't proclaim his strength; instead, he questions Jesus' identity.

The forerunner of the Messiah is afraid that he might have been wrong about Jesus. So he sent people to the right person. In Matthew 11:2-3, we are told that "he sent his disciples to ask Jesus, 'Are you the Messiah we've been expecting, or should we keep looking for someone else?'"

If this moment of doubt was the only picture of John we had, we would think of him as a failure. But this isn't the only picture. Jesus says in verse 11 of Matthew 11, "I tell you the truth, of all who have ever lived, none is greater than John the Baptist."

The enemy is a specialist at capitalizing on our doubts. But John's example ought to encourage us. Doubts don't have to be the final description of our faith. Do what John did. Go to Jesus. And when you do, you will experience your doubts being eased and your faith becoming stronger!

Prayer

Jesus, I want to thank You for strengthening me when I doubt. Your presence and reassurance give me the courage to keep moving forward. Help me to trust in Your power and love, especially in moments of uncertainty. Amen.

61
TATTOOS

"See, I have written your name on the palms of my hands."
(Isaiah 49:16)

"So after you have suffered a little while, He will restore, support, and strengthen you, and He will place you on a firm foundation."
(1 Peter 5:10)

While I know many think tattoos are cool, I have some simple advice: be careful what you permanently put ink on your body. I once knew a guy who tattooed the love of his life's name on his bicep. The problem was that a few months later; he had a new love of his life…with a different name.

I'm not sure if the word *tattoo* would completely describe this verse, but I'm thankful for it. "See, I have written your name on the palms of my hands." (Isaiah 49:16) While my heart has often pursued other "loves of my life," I am thankful that my (and your) name is written in the palm of His hand. Every time He lifts His mighty hand to do something marvelous and miraculous, He sees our names.

My prayer for you is that in your moments of feeling alone, hurt, confused, or discouraged, you will see the reminder that He loves you so much that He has tattooed your name on the palm of His hand. And every time He raises His hand to work, He sees your name.

You are not alone. He sees your hurt, confusion, and discouragement. Perhaps that is why Peter, who had his fair share of confusion and discouragement, wrote, "So after you have suffered a little while, He will restore, support, and strengthen you, and He will place you on a firm foundation." (1 Peter 5:10)

∼

Prayer

I want am thankful that You know me so intimately that You know my weaknesses, yet You still choose to restore and strengthen me. Your deep understanding and love give me hope and courage. Help me to lean on Your strength and trust in Your restorative power in every aspect of my life. Amen.

∼

62

A WATER-SKIING LESSON

"But when I am afraid, I will put my trust in you."
(Psalm 56:3)

My first and only attempt to water ski was quite a learning experience. I was out on Fort Gibson Lake in Oklahoma with a group of high school friends. Two of us had never skied before, so we gave it a try.

They put me in the water with the skis attached to my feet and gave me the rope. They raced the motor and took off. Soon, slack built in the rope. The experienced water skiers forgot to tell me what to do when that happens. You are supposed to pull the slack towards you. But since I didn't know, when the slack in the rope went tight, it yanked me out of the water and face-first back into the water.

Oh, my friends also forgot to tell me another important bit of information. When you fall...let go of the rope. So, I held on tight. Because I didn't let go, the force of the boat pulling me dragged me downward, ever further under the water.

That day, I learned a great spiritual truth, although it is still difficult for me to apply it. Sometimes, if you want to survive, you have to let go. Psalm 56:3 says, "But when I am afraid, I will put my trust in you."

Many years have passed since my skiing experience, and I am still learning to let go of my fears, problems, and stresses and trust Him.

I pray you also discover that His faithfulness is greater than your problems. It is safe to let them go into His care.

∽

Prayer

Heavenly Father, thank You for being my rock and my refuge. Help me to let go and trust You completely when I am afraid. Your presence gives me peace and the courage to face my fears, knowing that You are always in control. Amen.

∽

63
SUPPOSE IT DID - SUPPOSE IT DIDN'T

"These things I have spoken unto you, that in me ye might have peace. In the world ye shall have tribulation: but be of good cheer; I have overcome the world."
(John 16:33, KJV)

I love this antidote from Winnie the Pooh. One day, Piglet, who worries about everything, and Pooh are walking through some trees in the Hundred Acre Forest. Piglet says to the bear, "Supposing a tree fell down, Pooh, when we were underneath it?" Pooh, after some very careful thought, replied: "Supposing it didn't." And then A. A. Milne, who wrote the Pooh stories, writes "Piglet was comforted by this." [1]

You get to choose which perspective you want to live from. Choices about what life throws at you seldom come, but you

---

[1]. Milne, A. A. (1928) The House at Pooh Corner. p. 131. New York: E.P. Dutton & Co.

always have a choice in how you react to it. Life can harden you and make you cynical, or you can choose to see the beauty and wonder in the world. It's up to you.

John 16:33 has become one of my favorite Bible verses because it deals with reality yet speaks with optimism. Jesus said, "In the world ye shall have tribulation." That is the reality of life. You may walk through a forest, and a tree may fall on you. But here is the overcoming promise: "But be of good cheer; I have overcome the world."

Life will inevitably hand you some lemons—that's just a fact of existence. But it isn't a given that you will make lemonade. You can easily sit with your lemons and complain about how unfair life is. Or you can choose to see the silver lining. Who knows, perhaps now you have an opportunity to get great at making lemonade! I can assure you of this, if you hear Jesus' promise, you, like Piglet, will be comforted by this.

Prayer

Even though I will have tribulations in this world, You have overcome the world. Your victory gives me hope and strength to face any challenge. Help me trust in Your power and find peace in Your words, knowing that You have already conquered everything I fear. Amen.

64
ASSUMPTIONS PREVENT THE MIRACULOUS

"Now unto him that is able to do exceeding abundantly above all that we ask or think, according to the power that worketh in us."
(Ephesians 3:20 KJV)

In his book, "The Seven Levels of Change: The Guide to Innovation in the World's Largest Corporations," Rolf Smith claims children ask 125 probing questions a day. If you've been with a six-year-old for over four hours recently, you may think he underestimated that amount. Smith also adds that adults only ask 6 questions per day. [1]

Somewhere along the line, we lose 119 questions. Mark Batterson writes in *The Grave Robber*: "At some point, most of us stop asking questions and start making assumptions. That is the day our imagination dies. It's also the day miracles stop

---

1. Smith, Rolf. (1997). *The Seven Levels of Change: The Guide to Innovation in the World*, p. 49. Arlington, TX: Tapestry Press.

happening. If you want to experience the miraculous, you need to quit making assumptions." [2]

Psychologists call this "Cognitive Entrenchment." This means we cannot see beyond what we have experienced. Another word for it is "being in a rut."

As a believer, we should never become entrenched in what is possible. According to Paul, we serve a God who can do "exceeding abundantly above all that we ask or think, according to the power that worketh in us." (Ephesians 3:20)

Today, I challenge you to stop allowing life to conform you to "the routine." Let's live each day asking, "What amazing thing does God want to do around me today?"

∼

Prayer

I know you desire to work in me to do exceedingly abundantly above all I can ask or think. Your power and creativity go beyond my wildest dreams. Help me trust in Your plans and believe in the incredible things You are doing in my life. Amen.

∼

---

2. Batterson, Mark. (2014) *Grave Robber: How Jesus Can Make Your Impossible Possible*, p. 129. Grand Rapids: Baker Books

65

THE APPLE OF HIS EYE

"Keep me as the apple of your eye...."
(Psalm 17:8 NIV)

Several years ago, one of my granddaughters was sitting in my lap, looking intently into my eyes. I asked her what she was looking at, thinking she had this amazing affection for me that caused her to look lovingly into my eyes. She replied, "I can see myself in your eye." As she looked at me, she could see her reflection in the dark pupil of my eye. So much for that loving affection. And another example of children's brutal honesty.

The Psalmist petitioned God: "Keep me as the apple of your eye...." (Psalm 17:8) The ancient Hebrew idiom "apple of your eye" literally translates to "little man of the eye." [1] It's that reflection you can see of yourself in the pupil of someone's eye

---

[1]. BibleHub. (n.d.) "Strong's Hebrew: 380." https://biblehub.com/hebrew/380.htm.

when you are really close to them. But that is the key phrase... you must be really close to them!

Being the apple of someone's eye means you are very dear and important to them. It means being cherished and loved. And that's exactly how God feels about us!

When the Psalmist requests, "Keep me as the apple of your eye," he reminds us that God desires to be so close to us we can see our own reflection in His eyes. That's how close He wants to be to you today!

∼

Prayer

Heavenly Father, thank you for being so close to me that I am the apple of Your eye, the little man in Your sight. Your tender love and care mean everything to me. Help me to always remember how precious I am to You and to live in a way that reflects Your love. Amen.

∼

66

COMPLAINING

"Do everything without complaining and arguing, so that no one can criticize you."
(Philippians 2:14)

If you have ever sat at a Little League baseball or softball field, you have heard it. Angry parents, berating an umpire because they dared call Johnny out or Suzy's pitch a ball. On the college and professional level, it is not unusual to hear crowds chant obscenities in unison to show their displeasure with a referee.

According to the AP News Service, in June 2023, one New Jersey Little League director had enough. After two umpires quit because of parents' behavior, the director wrote and posted an updated code of ethics. Parents who verbally abuse umpires must umpire for three games, or they will face a one-year ban from the complex. To serve as an umpire, they must attend a three-hour training session, go through a concussion protocol course, and pass a background check.

I like that! I can think of other situations where this non-complaining ban could be effective. If you complain about the temperature at church, you are responsible for setting it to everyone's liking for three Sundays. Good luck with that. If you fuss about the songs in the worship set this week? You get to pick your choices for the next three weeks, along with the complaints about "too slow, too fast, too new, too old, too loud."

Of course, we could just heed the words of Paul in Philippians 2:14, "Do everything without complaining and arguing, so that no one can criticize you."

∼

Prayer

Thank You for all the blessings You've given me. Help me to guard against complaining and to always find reasons to be grateful. Remind me to focus on Your goodness and grace, even in challenging times, and to speak words that reflect a thankful heart. Amen.

∼

67

THE LIFTER OF MY HEAD

"But I have prayed for thee, that thy faith fail not: and when thou art converted, strengthen thy brethren."
(Luke 22:32, KJV)

"But thou, O LORD, art a shield for me; My glory, and the lifter up of mine head."
(Psalm 3:3 KJV)

~

In January 2019, the UCLA Bruins were playing basketball against the hometown Oregon Ducks. For 35 minutes, the Ducks had dominated the game, leading by as many as 17 points in the 2nd half. But UCLA fought back, and with only two minutes left, they had shrunk the deficit to 2 and had the ball. When the Ducks put pressure on the ball, UCLA threw it to their Freshman center, Moses Brown. Not accustomed to handling the ball, he wanted to get rid of it quickly. He did. He threw it straight out of bounds.

The Los Angeles Times records the play this way: "The possession had been lost, and maybe the game, as Moses Brown sulked his way back on defense. Head down, shoulders slumped, the UCLA freshman center had just thrown the ball out of bounds.... As the Ducks prepared to inbound the ball, Bruins point guard Jaylen Hands walked over to his teammate and slapped his hand before quickly, but tenderly, placing that same hand under Brown's chin and tilting it upward." [1]

In predicting one of the most public failures ever made (we are still reading and talking about it 2100 years later. And you thought yours was bad), Jesus told Simon Peter, "But I have prayed for thee, that thy faith fail not: and when thou art converted, strengthen thy brethren." (Luke 22:32) Rather than reprimand Peter for the coming failure, Jesus told him He was praying for him. Then, He put His hand under Peter's chin, raised it, and said, "When you are converted...." What a great example of Christian compassion we should follow. It gives new meaning to Psalm 3:3, doesn't it? "But thou, O Lord, art...the lifter of my head."

If you are hearing the groans of others from a past failure or mistake, take comfort. He will come to you and lift your chin as well.

By the way, UCLA won the game by three in overtime.

Prayer

Father, I thank You for encouraging me when I fail. Your love and support lift me up and give me the strength to try again. Help me always

---

1. Bolch, Ben. (January 11, 2019) *"UCLA Stuns Oregon with Incredible Comeback Victory"* Los Angeles Times. https://www.latimes.com/sports/ucla/la-sp-ucla-oregon-comeback-20190111-story.html

turn to You for encouragement and remember that Your grace is sufficient for all my shortcomings. Amen.

∼

68

WRESTLING BEARS

"Don't be afraid, for I am with you. Don't be discouraged, for I am your God. I will strengthen you and help you."
(Isaiah 41:10)

In May 2023, the Salem, Missouri, police department made the following post on their Facebook page:

> "Earlier this morning, we received phone calls about a black bear near Rolla Road. The Police Department closely monitored the situation, and the bear was last seen heading North back out of town. If you see or encounter a bear, please notify the Police Department, do not try and feed or interact with the bear. Thank you!"
> *REMINDER…AND YES, THIS IS REAL*
> "Please do not wrestle the bear if you come in contact. Bear

Wrestling is illegal in the state of Missouri per statute 578.176."[1]

I don't know about you, but I don't need a law declaring bear wrestling illegal to keep me from wrestling a bear that I meet in the wild. In real life, however, I sometimes don't get the choice of wrestling the bears of discouragement, disillusionment, and fear. I certainly wouldn't choose those wrestling matches on purpose. But you don't always get the choice. Something happens, and you find yourself in a wrestling match mentally, emotionally, and spiritually.

I am thankful that it is in those moments I hear Him say, "Don't be afraid, for I am with you. Don't be discouraged, for I am your God. I will strengthen you and help you." (Isaiah 41:10)

If you are wrestling with the bears of life, listen for His voice. He will be there to whisper, "Don't be afraid. I am with you."

∼

Prayer:

Your presence comforts me when I am afraid, disillusioned, or discouraged. Your nearness brings peace and reassurance to my troubled heart. Help me always seek Your presence and find solace in knowing You are with me every step of the way. Amen.

∼

---

1. Oberholtz, Chris. (June 1, 2023) *"It's Illegal to Wrestle Bears in Missouri, Police Warn After Multiple Sightings."* Fox Weather. https://www.foxweather.com/earth-space/bear-sighting-missouri-laws-prohibit-wrestling

69
LORD OF THE FRIES

"The silver is mine, and the gold is mine"
(Haggai 2:8)

Several years ago, I took one of my granddaughters to a local fast-food place for lunch. I had eaten a late breakfast, so I wasn't hungry. I ordered a soft drink and got her a kid's meal. As we sat eating, I took one of her fries. She was so upset with me because I stole one of her fries. She said, "Stop it! Those are mine!"

I thought, "Little girl, you don't understand who I am! I am the source of all your fries! I can take away all of your fries! I can smother you in fries! In fact, I am the Lord of the fries!" I probably should add that she was only four years old, so we can excuse her selfishness.

But I wonder how often I do the same thing to God. He asks me for a portion of finances, time, or talent, and I say, "Stop it! It's mine." But I'm not four years old. I so often need to be reminded that He gave me everything in the first place: my finances, my time, and my talents. He can take it all away or smother me with them.

The Lord reminds us in Haggai 2:8, "The silver is mine, and the gold is mine." (Haggai 2:8) When I act like my four-year-old granddaughter, He responds that it all belongs to Him. As Corrie Ten Boom once said, "Hold everything in your hands lightly. Otherwise, it hurts when God pries your fingers open." [1]

Prayer

∽

Heavenly Father, I am so blessed and I thank you for your provisions. Help me be generous, remembering that everything I have comes from You in the first place. Fill my heart with gratitude and a willingness to share Your gifts with others. Amen.

∽

---

1. Swindoll, Charles (1987) *Living Above the Level of Mediocrity: A Commitment to Excellence*, p. 114. Dallas, TX: Word Publishing

70
FEELING HOMESICK

"When you believed, you were marked in Him with a seal, the promised Holy Spirit, who is a deposit guaranteeing our inheritance until the redemption of those who are God's possession."
(Ephesians 1:13, 14, NIV)

∼

When I was the Head of School at Hamilton Heights Christian Academy, I received a phone call from a guidance counselor from a local high school. They had a new exchange student from Tanzania who was struggling. She called me when she discovered we had several students at Hamilton Heights from West African countries. The counselor said, "She's a little homesick and just wants to talk to someone from home." She wanted to know if she could come over and visit with our students... "just to hear from home."

So, the next day, we connected...a girl from Tanzania, two girls from Nigeria, a tall guy from Coweta, OK, and a guidance counselor from Chattanooga, TN. She just wanted to hear from home. She had been a little overwhelmed, but hearing from someone from home encouraged her.

I know how she felt. There are moments when life can be a little overwhelming. Sometimes I feel like a stranger in another country. Because I am. As a redeemed child of God, I belong to the Kingdom of Heaven. And, sometimes, I just long to hear from home. Ephesians 1:13-14 says: "When you believed, you were marked in Him with a seal, the promised Holy Spirit, who is a deposit guaranteeing our inheritance until the redemption of those who are God's possession."

When I feel like a stranger in another country, the Holy Spirit whispers, "Everything's okay. The Father guarantees your inheritance. Keep going. Keep living. One day, you'll be home."

Prayer

Jesus, I thank You for the promise of heaven and the hope it brings. Sometimes I feel so homesick for that eternal place with You. Help me to live each day with my heart set on heaven, longing for the day when I'll be with You forever. Amen.

71

UNCERTAINTIES

"Faith is the confidence that what we hope for will actually happen; it gives us assurance about things we cannot see."
(Hebrews 11:1)

"Are you sure this is going to work?" If I have heard that question once, I have heard it a hundred times during my adult life. And the obvious answer most of the time is: "No." Marketing guru Seth Godin reminds us of how often we have to make decisions while uncertain about the outcome. Godin writes: "100% certainty is not a variation of 96% or even 99%...Certainty is binary, yes or no. The question, 'Are you sure it will work?' is not about the work; it's about the sure...Some people go to work or school and do nothing except the things that they are sure about. The other path is to do things that might not work." [1]

1.

While I like certainty as much as the next person, the older I get, the more I realize very few things in life are certain. Isn't that what faith is all about? I often wonder how many amazing things I have missed seeing God do because I wouldn't take the step of faith because of a lack of certainty.

The great statement of faith in Hebrews 11:1 declares the way I want to finish my race: "Faith is the confidence that what we hope for will actually happen; it gives us assurance about things we cannot see." Hope for, and things we cannot see are not certainties. But it is faith. And verse 6 of Hebrews 11 adds: "And it is impossible to please God without faith."

Genuine faith embraces uncertainty, stepping beyond the sure into the extraordinary God has in store.

∼

Prayer

Jesus, I often face uncertainties in life, but I know they open doors of possibility for You to do extraordinary things. Your plans are greater than anything I can imagine. Help me trust in the opportunities that come with uncertainty and to believe that You are guiding me through every unknown. Amen.

∼

72

BEYOND THE MUNDANE

"Commit your actions to the Lord, and your plans will succeed."
(Proverbs 16:3)
"With God's help we will do mighty things!"
(Psalm 60:12)

~

During the beginning of the space race, on June 16, 1963, Soviet cosmonaut Valentina Tereshkova became the first woman in space and the only woman to fly solo in space. She had received very little formal education and began her work career in a textile factory. But she loved to skydive, and because of her expertise with a parachute, the Soviet space agency selected her to be a cosmonaut. She once said, "Anyone who has spent any time in space will love it for the rest of their lives. I achieved my childhood dream of the sky." Little did she know that her dream of the sky would carry her to the far reaches of space! [1]

God has a unique purpose for each of our lives. Sometimes, we may seem stuck in something mundane and frivolous, but we should never forget that He will help us discover our purpose and guide our steps in fulfilling that purpose. Proverbs 16:3 encourages us to "Commit your actions to the Lord, and your plans will succeed." I may not know God's purpose for your life, but here's what I know about that purpose. He has designed it, and He designs nothing frivolously. You are on planet Earth at this time, in this location, for a reason. Don't let the mundaneness of the moment dull your vision of His purpose for your life.

While I do not know Tereshkova's spiritual beliefs, her legacy has inspired many people to pursue their purpose and break through barriers. With the help of God, we can accomplish extraordinary things. May each of us rise today and declare with David, "With God's help we will do mighty things!" (Psalm 60:12)

∼

Prayer

Father, I thank You for Your amazing strength and guidance. With Your help, I know I can do mighty things. Fill me with Your power and courage to accomplish great works for Your glory. Amen.

∼

---

1. Lea, Robert. (September 4, 2023) "Valentina Tereshkova: First Woman in Space," Space.com. https://www.space.com/21571-valentina-tereshkova.html

🙞 73 🙜
GREATER IS HE THAT IS IN YOU

"Stay alert! Watch out for your great enemy, the devil. He prowls around like a roaring lion, looking for someone to devour."
(1 Peter 5:8)
"You have already won a victory...greater is He that is in you than He that it is the world."
(1 John 4:4)

Lions hunt in packs, with the females doing most of the work. They understand how their prey behaves and have developed practical strategies — like using the sound of fear trapping their targets. The oldest female lion is typically missing teeth and lacks speed and agility. Thus, she serves as the decoy because she has the loudest and most powerful roar of all. The pack hangs behind, secluded from sight, as the older female stays in front, seemingly alone, roaring. When the prey hears that roar, it often scatters toward the trees, running away from the perceived fear directly into the pack of eagerly awaiting lions. These lions use the power of fear, destroying their prey. [1]

Understanding that truth helps us understand what Peter wrote, "Stay alert! Watch out for your great enemy, the devil. He prowls around like a roaring lion, looking for someone to devour." (1 Peter 5:8) Could it be that when he roars in our lives, he is trying to chase us into the trees of disobedience, mistrust, and fear? Could it be that he knows he cannot defeat us because his fangs have been removed? Could it be that his roar causes us, in our fear, to fall prey to sin?

While he prowls and roars, may we never forget that Jesus, through his death and resurrection, defanged our great enemy. He took away the keys to death and the grave. May we always remember the words of John, "You have already won a victory... greater is he that is in you than he that it is the world." (1 John 4:4)

Prayer

Jesus, I know you are greater than any threat I face, especially when Satan, like a roaring lion, seeks to harm me. Your power and protection are my shield. Help me stand firm in faith, knowing that You are always greater and have already won the victory. Amen.

---

1. Roaring Realms. (n.d.) *"Lioness Leadership: Hunting Strategies."* https://roaringrealms.com/lioness-leadership-hunting-strategies

74
KEEPING ROWING...HE'S COMING

"He saw that they were in serious trouble, rowing hard and struggling against the wind and waves. About three o'clock in the morning Jesus came toward them, walking on the water. He intended to go past them,"
(Mark 6:48)

∽

My first cruise almost became my last one. I am prone to a little motion sickness, but I thought I could handle a cruise to Cozumel with about forty students and faculty from Hamilton Heights Christian Academy many years ago. I did fine... until the second night. A tropical storm south of our ship was churning up the waters. During the evening meal, we were swaying back and forth, but I was doing fine...until student after student, kept coming up and saying, "Mr. Stone, I'm getting sick." After about fifteen of their testimonies of nausea, I got it. Bad. (I'll leave it there). Amazing how others can affect you.

As I explore the miracle of Jesus walking on the water, a

small phrase in Matthew 14:24 (ESV) says that the boat was "...beaten by the waves struck me."

I've been there, haven't you? Sometimes, life can just beat you. But I love a little phrase in Mark's account of this story. Mark 6:48: "He saw they were in serious trouble...." That's right, while they were being beaten by the waves, Jesus saw them! And He sees you too.

What an incredible picture this is of Jesus' love and care for us! Even during our struggles and storms, Jesus sees us and comes to us. He doesn't wait for us to call out to him or to figure things out on our own. He actively comes to us, walking on the water to reach us in our time of need. And just as He walked the waters to their rescue, He is walking your way as well. "Peace, be still" is just a few moments away. Keep rowing...He's coming.

Prayer:

Jesus, thank You for showing up in the storms of my life, just like You did for the disciples. Your presence brings peace and calms my fears. Help me to trust that You are with me in every storm, guiding and protecting me through it all. Amen.

75

THIS SEASON WILL COME TO AN END

"Don't you realize that in a race everyone runs, but only one person gets the prize? So run to win! All athletes are disciplined in their training. They do it to win a prize that will fade away, but we do it for an eternal prize."
(1 Corinthians 9:24-25)

On Saturday, April 15, 2023, the University of Florida gymnast Trinity Thomas scored a perfect 10 at the NCAA Women's Gymnastics National Championship. According to bleacherreport.com, it wasn't her first 10. She actually tied the NCAA record for the most perfect scores in a Division 1 career with 28. After the competition, Thomas said, "I'm going to miss gymnastics so much. But I couldn't be more thankful." [1]

---

1. Rosa, Francisco (April 15, 2023) *"Florida's Trinity Thomas Ties NCAA Gymnastics Record with 28 Career Perfect 10s."* Bleacher Report. https://bleacherreport.com/articles/10072532-floridas-trinity-thomas-ties-ncaa-gymnastics-record-with-28-career-perfect-10s

Thomas' accomplishments are to be lauded. But they should also remind us of an important truth...all good things end. There will always be a Solomon to follow David, a Joshua to follow Moses, and an Elisha to follow Elijah.

When we are in a season of service, it is easy to forget that at some point, that season will end. May Thomas' statement remind us that our current role is only temporary. We will have our season in that role, then someone else will step in and the process will continue. Our time will come when we look back like she did, and say, "I'm going to miss _____ so much."

May we, like Thomas, always give our best during our season so that we can look back and say with her, "I couldn't be more thankful."

∽

Prayer:

Heavenly Father, thank You for the season of service You've given me. I know that this time will eventually end, and someone else will step in to continue Your work. Help me serve faithfully now and trust that You will guide and empower those who come after me to carry on Your mission. Amen.

∽

76

FIGHTING AGAINST MYSELF

"Better to be patient than powerful; better to have self-control than to conquer a city."
(Proverbs 16:32)

One morning, during my devotional time, I observed an Eastern bluebird fiercely attacking a door's glass panes. I am told this behavior stems from their territorial nature. The bird sees its reflection as an intruder and defends its territory. After a few clashes, it flew away, only to return and restart the confrontation. Its bird brain (pun intended) couldn't grasp that it was fighting with itself.

I wonder how often I am like that bluebird. It's easy to assume that others are the source of my troubles. However, I've learned that usually, the source of my frustration is…myself. The interpersonal challenges I face are reflections of the insecurities within my heart.

I pray for the wisdom to recognize these reflections and

allow His Spirit to guide me on my journey to Christlikeness. Proverbs 16:32 says, "Better to be patient than powerful; better to have self-control than to conquer a city." I desire to cultivate patience, self-control, and inner peace that transcends life's conflicts.

When I acknowledge my insecurities, I open the door for the Holy Spirit to work in my life to help me overcome them. When I take responsibility for my own actions and attitudes, the Spirit can begin His work of transforming me into the image of Christ.

That bluebird, engaged in its seemingly endless struggle, taught me that self-reflection is essential in my pursuit of being like Jesus. Instead of blaming other people or circumstances, I can confess my failures, find forgiveness through His grace, and let His Spirit empower me to overcome my weaknesses.

∼

Prayer

Father, I need your help in overcoming my insecurities. Your love and strength give me confidence and peace. Help me trust in Your view of me and rise above my doubts, knowing that You have equipped me for every good work. Help me stop fighting against myself. Amen.

∼

77
A SWEETER SONG

"Run from anything that stimulates youthful lusts. Instead, pursue righteous living...."
(2 Timothy 2:22)

"Fix your thoughts on what is true, and honorable, and right, and pure, and lovely, and admirable. Think about things that are excellent and worthy of praise."
(Philippians 4:8)

∼

In the Greek classic *Odyssey*, Jason and his sailing crew, the Argonauts encounter the Sirens, who use their irresistible songs to lure sailors to shipwreck and death. Following the advice of Circe, the sorceress, Jason plugs the ears of his crew with beeswax so that they cannot hear the Sirens' song.

However, Jason wants to experience the temptation of the Sirens' song, so he has himself tied to the ship's mast. When he hears the music, he commands the sailors to set him free and to sail to what would be their doom. By plugging their ears and binding him, they keep the ship and crew safe. Jason demonstrates one way to deal with temptation. By being proactive and employing a combination of self-restraint and practical measures, the crew of the *Argo* remained safe. It reminds me of what Paul told Timothy, "Run from anything that stimulates youthful lusts. Instead, pursue righteous living...." (2 Timothy 2:2)

In contrast, in Apollonius of Rhodes' story, *Argonautica*, Orpheus, a legendary musician and poet, takes a more creative approach to dealing with the temptresses. When his crew encountered the Sirens, Orpheus played his lyre and used his musical talent to counteract the Siren's tempting song. Because his tune was sweeter, he drowned out the Sirens' song, enabling the crew to sail past the danger. This is what the Apostle Paul encourages in Philippians 4:8 when he writes, "Fix your thoughts on what is true, and honorable, and right, and pure, and lovely, and admirable. Think about things that are excellent and worthy of praise."

Both Jason and Orpheus demonstrate the importance of being aware of one's vulnerabilities and taking appropriate actions to resist temptation.

We can focus on the danger, the snares, and the ugliness of sin, and take actions to prevent their infringement on our lives. But there is another way to overcome the temptations of the enemy. Rather than listen to the siren's song of seduction, we can tune our ears to the sweeter song of God's love. I am convinced that there is a victory that can be found, not in avoiding the world, but being tuned in to the heavenly.o When we really hear His song, no song of seduction can lure us to destruction. The sound of the Savior's grace will overwhelm any temptress song.

Prayer

Lord, thank You for Your amazing blessings that draw me closer to You. Help me focus more on the joy and fulfillment Your blessings bring than on avoiding the dangers of sin. Lord, may Your goodness captivate my heart and guide me to live a life that honors and pleases You. Amen.

∽

78

FAITHFUL THROUGH CHANGE

"There went with us also certain of the disciples of Cæsarea, and brought with them one Mnason of Cyprus, an old disciple, with whom we should lodge."
(Acts 21:16)

The book of Acts offers an insightful glance into the lives of many believers who played a pivotal role in the growth and development of the early Christian church. Acts 21:16 mentions Mnason as one of those individuals. "There went with us also certain of the disciples of Cæsarea, and brought with them one Mnason of Cyprus, an old disciple, with whom we should lodge." The New Living Translation says Manson was one of the early disciples of Jesus. The events of Acts 21 took place almost 30 years after the death, resurrection, and ascension of Jesus.

Think of all the changes Mnason witnessed when he was a young believer. The church moved from being a predominantly Jewish constituency to reaching Gentiles with their various customs and values. The Jerusalem Council shifted some long-standing traditions of the Jewish believers to acceptance of things they once thought were unacceptable. There was conflict in churches at Corinth, Philippi, and in the providence of Galatia.

Yet, Mnason remained faithful. He didn't become passive because of the changes; instead, in his old age, he was still doing what he could by providing lodging for Paul and his friends.

It is only natural as we age to become nostalgic about how it used to be. But let's follow the example of Mnason, remain faithful, and continue to minister in the ways we can.

Prayer

Father, I thank You for Your steadfast love and presence in my life. Help me remain faithful to You, even when I experience a lot of change. Give me the strength and courage to trust in Your unchanging nature, knowing that You are with me through every transition. Amen.

79
OWNING UP OR LOSING OUT

"I am sorry that I ever made Saul king, for he has not been loyal to me and has refused to obey my command."
(1 Samuel 15:11)

Natalie Neysa Alund reported in USA Today about a driver stopped in Springfield, Colorado, on suspicion of drunk driving. As the officer approached his vehicle, the driver switched seats with his dog. When confronted, the man claimed he was not driving. It was the dog.¹

Blame-shifting is a psychological defense mechanism where individuals attempt to shift responsibilities for their actions, mistakes, or adverse consequences. An extreme example is an attempt to blame your dog for driving intoxicated.

---

1. Alund, Natalie Neysa. (May 15, 2023) *"Driver Switches Seats with Dog to Avoid DUI Arrest, Colorado Police Say."* USA Today. https://www.usatoday.com/story/news/nation/2023/05/15/colorado-dui-dog-drivers-seat/70221021007/

A verse of Scripture has intrigued me concerning King Saul, "I am sorry that I ever made Saul king, for he has not been loyal to me and has refused to obey my command." (1 Samuel 15:11). I have wondered what Saul did that so wrong, that God repented?

As I explore his downfall, it becomes clear that Saul tended to blame someone else for his troubles. Once, it was because Samuel was late in offering sacrifices. He often complained that David was more popular. Saul's blame-shifting went on and on until the anointing left him, and he lost the kingdom. But perhaps most tragically, God repented He had ever used him.

Unlike Saul, David, when confronted by the prophet Nathaniel concerning his sins with Bathsheba and Uriah, accepted responsibility and, in Psalm 51, confessed his failures. God Himself described David as a man after His own heart. I must ask myself, "Who do I want my life to reflect, the one rejected by God or the one forgiven by God?"

Prayer

Heavenly Father, thank You for Your grace and forgiveness. Help me not to blame others for my failures, but to accept responsibility and repent. Give me the strength to own my mistakes and seek Your guidance in making things right, trusting in Your mercy and love. Amen.

❧ 80 ☙
BIRDS' SONGS

"Let all that I am praise the Lord. O Lord my God, how great you are! You are robed with honor and majesty."
(Psalm 104:1)

"The birds nest beside the streams and sing among the branches of the trees."
(Psalm 104:12)

Photography is one of my hobbies, and I love shooting pictures of the beautiful birds in nature. Did you know that according to Research Reports last year, two independent scientific research projects provided data that indicates seeing or hearing birds sing can be good for your mental and emotional well-being? The study shows that listening to birds helps to reduce anxiety, depression, and paranoia. In fact, for patients diagnosed with clinical depression, the songs of birds provided relief even when other, more conventional measures offered little help. [1]

The Psalmist declares in Psalm 104:1, "Let all that I am praise the Lord. O Lord my God, how great you are! You are robed with honor and majesty." He then describes the many ways nature exalts and magnifies the Lord. "The birds nest beside the streams and sing among the branches of the trees." (verse 12) Every element of creation, from the smallest twig to the largest forest, joins in a chorus of praise, celebrating the majesty of the Creator.

Perhaps that is one reason the songs of our feathered friends have such a therapeutic impact on our emotional well-being. As they sing their songs to glorify the Creator, they invite us to join and declare His majesty. May we hear their invitation and lift our hearts to declare His majesty!

Prayer

Heavenly, Father, I am overwhelmed by the beauty of Your creation. I join with all of creation in praising You, lifting my voice and heart in worship. Let every part of my life reflect Your glory and honor You as the Creator of all things. Amen.

---

1. Sima, Richard. (May 18, 2024) *"How Birdsong Can Transform Our Mental Health."* The Washington Post. https://www.washingtonpost.com/wellness/interactive/2023/birds-song-nature-mental-health-benefits/

81

FACING THE STORM

"When you go THROUGH deep waters, I will be with you. When you go THROUGH rivers of difficulty, you will not drown. When you walk THROUGH the fire of oppression, you will not be burned up; the flames will not consume you."
(Isaiah 43:2)

According to a January 23, 2015, article in *The Tennesseean* newspaper, cows and buffaloes have entirely different ways of facing storms. The author, Rory Vaden, states that when cows sense a storm coming, they move in the opposite direction from the oncoming storm, running AWAY from it. The cows move with the storm and actually prolong the storm's impact.

Buffaloes, according to Vaden, do something unique. When they sense an oncoming storm, they turn and charge INTO it.

Instead of running with the storm, they run through it, minimizing its impact. [1]

Perhaps that is why God tells us, "When you go THROUGH deep waters, I will be with you. When you go THROUGH rivers of difficulty, you will not drown. When you walk THROUGH the fire of oppression, you will not be burned up; the flames will not consume you." (Isaiah 43:2)

While we are all tempted to run from our storms, may we instead turn and face them with the promise of our Heavenly Father, "I will be with you." The storm's power is no match for the power of the Creator. If we truly believe Romans 8:28 and genuinely believe that He is in control and that no weapon formed against us shall prosper, then, rather than run from our storms, we can turn into them, knowing He is with us!

Prayer

"You are my strength in the storms of life. Help me to face every challenge with courage, knowing that You are with me. With Your help, I can go through any storm, trusting in Your guidance and protection. Amen.

---

1. Vaden, Rory (January 23, 2015) *"Be the Buffalo and Face Life's Storms."* The Tennessean. https://www.tennessean.com/story/money/2015/01/23/buffalo-face-lifes-storms/22187351/

82
WHO IS YOUR SWIM BUDDY

"Two people are better off than one, for they can help each other succeed. If one person falls, the other can reach out and help. But someone who falls alone is in real trouble. A person standing alone can be attacked and defeated, but two can stand back-to-back and conquer. Three are even better, for a triple-braided cord is not easily broken."
(Ecclesiastes 4: 9-10, 12)

In his 2023 book, *The Wisdom of the Bullfrog: Leadership Made Simple (But Not Easy)*, Retired U.S. Navy Admiral William H. McRaven writes, "The greatest compliment one frogman can bestow on another is to call him 'a swim buddy.' It's a simple term, but it conveys everything about how we live, how we fight, and sometimes how we die." [1]

Richard M. Charette, Chief of Staff for Wells Fargo Digital

---

1. McRaven, William H. (2023). The Wisdom of the Bullfrog, p. 259. New York: Grand Central Publishing

Research and Strategy, adds about swim buddies in his 2020 article, "There is no such a thing as a 'half-a-swim-buddy'. A swim buddy is there and has your back, all the time, or he's not.... Your swim buddy is not your lifeguard: he's your partner." [2]

A grad-school professor once told our class of counseling psychology students, "If each of us had just one person with whom we could share everything, there would be no need for therapists."

Let me remind you of the words of the wise man in Ecclesiastes 4:9-10, 12, "Two people are better off than one, for they can help each other succeed. If one person falls, the other can reach out and help. But someone who falls alone is in real trouble. A person standing alone can be attacked and defeated, but two can stand back-to-back and conquer. Three are even better, for a triple-braided cord is not easily broken."

Who is your swim buddy?

∽

Prayer

Father, thank You for the gift of godly relationships. Help me cherish and nurture these connections, knowing their importance in my life. Surround me with people who can support me when I'm struggling. Help me be a source of strength and encouragement for them as well. Amen.

∽

---

2. Charette, Richard M. (May 15, 2020) *"We All Need a Swim Buddy."* LinkedIn. https://www.linkedin.com/pulse/we-all-need-swim-buddy-richard-m-charette

83
THE POWER OF SONG

"But I will sing of Your strength, in the morning I will sing of Your love; for You are my fortress, my refuge in times of trouble. You are my strength, I sing praise to You; You, God, are my fortress, my God on whom I can rely."
(Psalm 59:16, 17 NIV)

A marketing study in Sweden indicates that playing background music during the week boosted customers spending on Monday through Thursday. It didn't have the same impact on the weekend. What was the difference?

"On the weekdays, people tend to be more mentally and physically depleted," says co-author Carl-Philip Ahlbom, a senior lecturer at the University of Bath's School of Management in England. In such a state, he explains, shoppers tend to use intuitive processing, rather than active reasoning, making them more receptive to the relaxing effects of music. The music causes them to linger longer in the store, look more, and ultimately buy more items, he says. The idea, according to Ahlbom, is that music makes people feel better when they are depleted and often encourages them to continue shopping. [1]

In the Bible, David's music calmed Saul's troubled spirit (1 Samuel 16:14-23). Before departing the Last Supper, Jesus and the disciples sang a hymn before He entered the Garden of Gethsemane and the agony of His prayer of submission (Matthew 26:30). In Psalm 59:16, 17, David testifies, "But I will sing of Your strength, in the morning I will sing of Your love; for You are my fortress, my refuge in times of trouble. You are my strength, I sing praise to You; You, God, are my fortress, my God on whom I can rely."

If you are feeling depleted, let me encourage you to sing praise to the God who is your strength!

Prayer
Father, I thank You for the gift of song. Help me lift my voice in praise, especially when I'm going through difficulties. Let my songs of worship bring comfort and strength, reminding me of Your presence and faithfulness. Amen.

---

[1]. Ahlbom, Carl-Philip, et al. (2023) "Understanding How Music Influences Shopping on Weekdays and Weekends." Journal of Marketing Research 60, no. 5 (2023): 987-1007. doi:10.1177/00222437221150930.

❧ 84 ❧
THE BIRD'S POINT OF VIEW

"Rejoice with those who rejoice, weep with those who reap."
(Romans 12:15)

Caroll Spinney was the actor and puppeteer who, beginning in 1969, played the original Big Bird on Sesame Street for decades. In his 2003 memoir, *"The Wisdom of Big Bird (And the Dark Genius of Oscar the Grouch",* Spinney says that the original costume was so cumbersome that he could not see where he was going while he was in it. Because he had to perform without being able to see, he would often stumble over things, bump into walls, and walk off-camera in the wrong direction.

Finally, using late 1960s technology, the producers rigged a tiny television monitor inside his suit. Spinney wrote, "The moment I had the monitor inside the Bird, my performances became much better. I had room in the puppet to look down at the tiny picture and see what Big Bird was doing. I see the same picture the viewer sees, not the world from the Bird's point of view." [1]

Bill Murphy, Jr. commented on this story, "In order to do his job, Spinney had to learn how to see the world constantly from other people's points of view." [2] This skill allowed him to connect deeply with others and understand their needs and emotions. By adopting diverse perspectives, he could create more meaningful and impactful work, fostering empathy and collaboration in his professional environment.

Isn't that what the church is to do? "Rejoice with those who rejoice, weep with those who weep." (Romans 12:15) I certainly think I can be more empathetic when I choose to see the world from their point of view, rather than from my perspective.

∽

Prayer

Jesus, the gift of empathy is crucial in helping others. Help me to truly share in the joys and sorrows of others, rejoicing when they rejoice and weeping when they weep. Give me a compassionate heart that seeks to understand and support those around me, reflecting Your love and care. Amen.

∽

---

1. Spinney, Caroll. (2003) *The Wisdom of Big Bird (and the Dark Genius of Oscar the Grouch): Lessons from a Life in Feathers,* p. 43. New York: Villard
2. Murphy Jr., Bill. (May 28, 2023) *"How People with High Emotional Intelligence Use the 'Big Bird Rule' to Become Exceptionally Successful."* Inc. https://www.inc.com/bill-murphy-jr/how-people-with-high-emotional-intelligence-use-big-bird-rule-to-become-exceptionally-successful.html

85

THE WHO IS MORE IMPORTANT THAN THE WHAT

"O Lord, how long will You forget me? Forever? How long will You look the other way? But I trust in Your unfailing love. I will rejoice because You have rescued me. I will sing to the Lord because He is good to me." (Psalm 13:1, 5, 6)

On "The Price Is Right" television game show, a contestant won a fantastic trip to Hawaii...and the emergency room. After winning the trip, Henry celebrated exuberantly, throwing his arms up and down and hopping around the stage.

When he returned to spin the big wheel, his wife, Alice, accompanied him. The host, Drew Carey, explained that Henry had dislocated his shoulder during his earlier celebration. His wife spun a fantastic number, and Carey turned to Henry and said, "Don't hurt yourself."[1]

Carey's comment reminded me of watching someone

---

1. Paige, Ashley. (June 20, 2023) *"The Price Is Right Contestant Dislocates Shoulder*

exuberantly worshiping with all their might. Someone would say, "I hope they don't hurt themselves." To which the obligatory response was, "If they're in the Spirit, they won't."

At times, the presence of the Lord has deeply moved me, overwhelming my emotions. I am thankful for those moments. There are other times when, like David, I have felt abandoned. "O Lord, how long will You forget me? Forever? How long will You look the other way?" (Psalms 13:1) At those times, I didn't feel like throwing my arms up and down in exuberant worship.

Both extremes have taught me an essential truth about worship. My worship is not dependent upon WHAT I am experiencing at the moment, but on WHO I am worshiping. In verses 5 and 6, David concluded, "But I trust in Your unfailing love. I will rejoice because You have rescued me. I will sing to the Lord because He is good to me." Regardless of my current situation, I have learned I can trust His unfailing love and sing of His goodness to me.

∼

Prayer

I worship You for who You are, not just for how I feel. Help me worship You based on Your unchanging nature and greatness, regardless of my emotions. Let my praise be constant and true, honoring You for Your character and love. Amen.

∼

Celebrating Winning a Trip to Hawaii." People. https://people.com/the-price-is-right-contestant-dislocates-shoulder-celebrating-7550047#:

86

IT'S GONNA BE A BRIGHT, SUNSHINY DAY

"I will sing to the Lord because he is good to me."
(Psalms 13:6)

For Hazel Hardy, missing her choir practice was unthinkable. Her choir met on Wednesdays in a London church. She would take the Tube (subway) or two city buses to rehearsals. Hazel said that by the time she arrived, she had "escaped whatever was outside," including her cancer. [1]

The choir met from 2016 to 2018. All the members were familiar with cancer, either patients, caregivers, or oncologists. But they didn't discuss the "c" word at choir rehearsal. They were there to sing and have some fun.

The Post article continued, "After rehearsals, some of the

---

1. Soong, Kelyn. (June 25, 2023) *"The Benefits of Singing with Others for Mental and Physical Health."* The Washington Post. https://www.washingtonpost.com/wellness/2023/06/25/singing-with-others-mental-physical-health/.

singers provided a saliva sample to researchers examining whether singing affected their health and mood — and it did, positively. The 'Sing With Us' study, which enrolled Hardy and 192 others, is part of a growing body of research on the physical and mental health benefits of singing with others. Other studies have found a connection between singing and lessened anxiety, stimulated memory for those with dementia, increased lung capacity, and an easing of postpartum depression."

The choir's first song was "I Can See Clearly Now." When one of the choir members died of cancer, they sang the song at her funeral:

> I think I can make it now, the pain is gone
> All of the bad feelings have disappeared
> Here is that rainbow I've been praying for
> It's gonna be a bright, bright, sunshiny day."[2]

It is no wonder the Psalmist declared, "I will sing to the Lord because he is good to me." (Psalms 13:6). Singing to the Lord will help you see clearly. And if you are brave enough, singing with someone makes it even better!

Prayer

Heavenly Father, I thank You for the ability to sing Your praises even during hardships. Help me lift my voice in song, finding strength and comfort in worship when times are tough. Let my heart be filled with Your joy and peace, turning every struggle into an opportunity to glorify You. Amen.

---

2. Nash, Johnny. (1972) "I Can See Clearly Now," Epic Records.

87

DON'T GIVE UP

"Demas has deserted me because he loves the things of this life and has gone to Thessalonica. Crescens has gone to Galatia, and Titus has gone to Dalmatia. Alexander the metalworker did me a great deal of harm.... At my first defense, no one came to my support, but everyone deserted me."
(2 Timothy 4:10, 14, 16, 18)

"So let's not get tired of doing what is good. At just the right time we will reap a harvest of blessing if we don't give up."
(Galatians 6:9)

~

From our current perspective, it's pretty easy to see Paul as one of the great winners in history. As such, it is nearly impossible to imagine Paul as a man who struggled with feelings of abandonment, discouragement, and despair.

And yet, that is almost certainly how he saw himself. Near the end of his life, Paul wrote letters from a prison cell to churches that seemed to be fragmenting. He felt abandoned by his friends. In what is believed to be his last letter before his death, he wrote to his young disciple, Timothy, and recounted how Demas had abandoned him and gone to Thessalonica because of Demas' love for this world. "Crescens has gone to Galatia, and Titus to Dalmatia." (2 Timothy 2: 10) And although Crescens and Titus had not deserted the Lord, they were not with Paul in these closing days of his life.

He continued in verses 14 and 16, "Alexander the metalworker did me a great deal of harm.... At my first defense, no one came to my support, but everyone deserted me." His only hope appeared to be in the afterlife. "The Lord will rescue me from every evil attack and will bring me safely to his heavenly kingdom." (verse 18) Without his faith, Paul must have seen his earthly work as a failure, destined to be forgotten. What we see today—at least two billion Christians—was probably unimaginable to him.

Paul's experiences ought to remind us that the things we are experiencing are only the seeds of future harvests. No wonder he would write in Galatians 6, "So let's not get tired of doing what is good. At just the right time we will reap a harvest of blessing if we don't give up." (Galatians 6:9) The keywords are, "Don't give up." Paul's words, and his experiences, remind us that "at just the right time," our faithfulness will "reap a harvest of blessing." So let me say it again, "Don't give up!"

Prayer

Jesus, I thank You for Your constant presence and love. Help me persevere, even when I feel abandoned by others. Strengthen my faith and resolve, reminding me that You will never leave me, and with You, I can endure any trial. Amen.

88
HIGHER GROUND

"If ye then be risen with Christ, seek those things which are above, where Christ sitteth on the right hand of God. Set your affection on things above, not on things on the earth.
(Colossians 3:1-2 KJV)

I was a young minister when I first heard the analogy between geese flying in the V formation and the church. When they fly together, their formation provides lift and reduces resistance for the geese following. They encourage each other with their honking. They rotate leadership so that another goose steps up to lead when the leader tires. Scientists have also discovered when one goose, because of illness or injury, drops out of the formation, two others join it to help on the journey!

However...

Having geese in my backyard, I have discovered that they are not nearly as congenial and supportive when they are not in the air flying. They are highly territorial. They snip at and pull the feathers from other geese who aren't a part of their immediate family. Their honking isn't for encouragement but warnings to stay away. I recently saw a goose in the water lower its head, stiffen its neck, and take off after a blue heron.

In the air, they live in a spirit of cooperation. On the ground, they war and fight. I guess it's just a matter of where you decide to live. When, as followers of Jesus, we "set our affections on things above" (Colossians 3:2), we live in unity, love, and the abiding presence of His Spirit. When we choose to live on an earthly plain, we quibble and argue about styles of music, the temperature in the sanctuary, and whether it is or isn't a move of God.

So, my heart cries the words of this old hymn,

> Lord, lift me up, and let me stand on higher ground.
> By faith, on heaven's tableland.
> A higher plain than I have found,
> Lord, plant my feet on higher ground. [1]

Prayer

God, You have called me to live above the entanglements of the world. Help me focus on You and rise above distractions and temptations. Give me the strength to live a life that honors You, staying true to Your path and purpose. Amen.

---

1. Oatman Jr., Jonathan. (1898) "Higher Ground," Music composed by Charles H. Gabriel. Published in *Songs of Love and Praise No. 5*. Philadelphia: John J. Hood

89

COMFORTED TO COMFORT

"He comforts us in all our troubles so that we can comfort others. When they are troubled, we will be able to give them the same comfort God has given us. For the more we suffer for Christ, the more God will shower us with His comfort through Christ."
(2 Corinthians 1:4, 5)

In his book *Strength To Strength: Finding Success, Happiness, and Deep Purpose in the Second Half of Life*, Albert Brooks talks about a friend from many years ago who was a clinical psychologist with a booming practice in New England.

At forty-five, he was at the top of his profession, which he adored. But he had a problem: having suffered all his life with type 1 diabetes, he was now losing his sight—not an uncommon malady for diabetics as they age. His initial reaction was total denial, and he insisted on continuing his life as he always had, including driving. He finally faced up to his impending blindness —averting potential tragedy—when his neighbors complained he was running over their mailboxes. He struggled for several years, angry at God for giving him this cruel fate.

But then, one day, he received a phone call from a woman who told him she was experiencing a mental health crisis and needed treatment but had a reason not to divulge her identity. She was quite famous and desired anonymity, even with her therapist. She needed—and found—a blind psychologist. He helped the woman and went on to build a practice around well-known people who desired similar treatment. [1]

The Apostle Paul tells us in 2 Corinthians 1:4, "He comforts us in all our troubles so that we can comfort others. When they are troubled, we will be able to give them the same comfort God has given us."

Most of us can testify as Paul did in verse 5, "For the more we suffer for Christ, the more God will shower us with his comfort through Christ." You never know when God will use the situation where you need His comfort to be a blessing to someone else.

∽

Prayer

Jesus, thank You for the comfort You have provided during my difficulties. Help me use the comfort I've received to support and comfort others who are struggling. Let Your love and compassion flow through me, bringing hope and healing to those in need. Amen.

∽

---

1. Brooks, Arthur C. (2022). *From Strength to Strength: Finding Success, Happiness, and Deep Purpose in the Second Half of Life*, p. 174. New York: Portfolio

90

SOMEBODY COME AND PLAY

Come now, and let us reason together, saith the LORD: though your sins be as scarlet, they shall be as white as snow; though they be red like crimson, they shall be as wool."
(Isaiah 1:18 KJV)

The Spirit and the bride say, 'Come.' Let anyone who hears this say, 'Come.' Let anyone who is thirsty come. Let anyone who desires drink freely from the water of life."
(Revelation 22:17)

"Come unto me, all ye that are weary and heavy laden, and I will give you rest."
(Matthew 11:28 KJV).

~

The creators of Sesame Street thought it would be great to let Big Bird tour the country and perform with some of the outstanding symphonies in different cities to teach children about the instruments in the orchestra. Their first show was in Hawaii with the Honolulu Symphony.

The first song in the program was "Somebody Come and Play." Caroll Spinney, who was the puppeteer for Big Bird, wrote, "I made a mistake. On a musical bridge in the middle of the song, I had the Bird plaintively say, 'Won't someone come and play with me?' Chaos! Children ran down the aisle, and about twenty-eight of them climbed up onstage and surrounded Big Bird. I was relieved that not one child attempted to pull a feather. After the song, the kids went back to their seats, and I made a mental note not to say that again." [1]

Have you ever noticed how often God says to us, "Come"? He says, "Come now, let us reason together." "The Spirit and the Bride say, "Come". "Let anyone who is thirsty, Come." And of course, "Come unto me, all ye that are weary and heavy laden, and I will give you rest." (Matthew 11:28).

Wouldn't it be amazing if we, like little children, heard the invitation and took off running for God? I don't even think He would mind if we pulled a feather or two. I know this: if we come, He will give us rest.

∽

Prayer

Heavenly Father, I thank You for inviting me to come to You. Help me accept Your invitation wholeheartedly, seeking Your presence and guidance. Let my life be a testament to the peace and joy found in drawing near to You. Amen.

∽

---

1. Spinney, Caroll. (2003) *The Wisdom of Big Bird (and the Dark Genius of Oscar the Grouch)*, pp. 98-100. New York: Villard

ACKNOWLEDGMENTS

∼

As you conclude these 90 days of seeing God's magnificence in life's small, ordinary things, I would like to thank you for allowing me to be a part of your pursuit of our extraordinary God. I never take lightly the responsibility of sharing God's Word with His most prized possession on this planet, His people. I consistently remind myself of the words of James when he wrote, "Dear brothers and sisters, not many of you should become teachers in the church, for we who teach will be judged more strictly." (James 3:1) Thank you again for joining in this journey.

I would also like to thank my wife, Shirlene, and my three children, Michael, Krystal, and Stephen, who have been a part of my ministry in many ways. They have loved me in good times, shown kindness to me when I didn't always model Christlikeness, and been a source of motivation for me in my desire to be faithful to my Savior, Jesus Christ.

My seven grandchildren (number 8 is on the way even as I write) have driven me to publish my books. For many years, many people have encouraged me to write a book. And to be honest, it was never on my bucket list. But not too long ago, I realized that writing a book would be the best way to leave my heart for Christ to my grandchildren. After I have preached my last sermon and written my last line, may this and any subsequent books encourage my family to continue pursuing my extraordinary God.

To my Church of God of Prophecy family, thank you for your friendship, encouragement, and support. Many have blessed and enriched me in the church world, but the tribe I have been a part of has been uniquely impactful. My church family has strengthened my faith, and I am deeply grateful for the community and belonging you provide. Each place of ministry I have been allowed to serve has contributed to my development and growth in Christ.

Of course, I always give thanks to the Magnificent One. I join the multitude of believers, past, present, and future, who desire to live out their lives to know Him in a greater and deeper way. His infinite wisdom and boundless love have guided me through every step of this journey, and His presence has been a constant source of strength and comfort.

ABOUT THE AUTHOR

∼

Duke and his wife Shirlene serve as the Regional Bishop in the Magnolia Region of Louisiana and Mississippi. Before assuming this role, they served as National Evangelists for the International Offices of the Churches of God of Prophecy. They also served as pastors in Indiana, Florida, and Tennessee.

Duke has a Master of Education degree from the University of Tennessee. He was the founder and Head of School for Hamilton Heights Christian Academy, a fully accredited high school in Chattanooga, TN. During his tenure as the Head of School, Hamilton Heights served students from the greater Chattanooga area and over 180 students from 30 different nations across North America, South America, Europe, Asia, Australia, and Africa. For over thirty years, Duke wrote high school and collegiate literature for the *One Accord* educational curriculum. He has authored two Bible studies for **spiritmatters** curriculum on the life of Moses and the life of Jonah.

Duke and Shirlene have three grown children: Michael and his wife, Ceren; Krystal and her husband, Jason; and Stephen, and his wife, Caitlyn. They have seven grandchildren with their eight coming soon.

UPCOMING BOOKS BY DUKE
STONE

∽

Coming in the Fall of 2024

The Tears Mean He's Real: A Fresh Look at the Death and Resurrection of Lazarus

Coming in early 2025

The Extraordinary Ordinary: Seeing The Magnificence of God in the Ordinary: Volume 2

Made in the USA
Columbia, SC
19 August 2024

40616155R00119